Women in Black History

Stories of Courage, Faith, and Resilience

Tricia Williams Jackson

Revell

a division of Baker Publishing Group
Grand Rapids, Michigan

Text © 2016 by Tricia Williams Jackson

Illustrations © 2016 by Tim Foley Illustration

Published by Revell
a division of Baker Publishing Group
P.O. Box 6287, Grand Rapids, MI 49516-6287
www.revellbooks.com

Printed in the United States of America

Library of Congress Cataloging-in-Publication Data is on file at the Library of Congress, Washington, DC.

978-0-8007-2652-2

Scripture is taken from the King James Version of the Bible.

Illustrations by Tim Foley, timfoleyillustration.com

16 17 18 19 20 21 22   7 6 5 4 3 2 1

Contents

A Word to the Reader

The fourteen African-American women you are about to meet were real women. They walked the same earth you and I walk, and they made their unique mark upon it. You've heard of some of them, and some of them will be new names to you. Several of them started their lives in slavery. Most started their lives in poverty. Some overcame both of those conditions, some overcame physical disability, some overcame obstacles put in their way by society.

The earliest woman in this book was born in 1753—before the American Revolution took place—and the most recent woman was born in 1940—before the Civil Rights movement made positive changes for African Americans. Each woman accomplished so much, particularly for the times in which she lived. Each in her own way believed in God's plan for her life—the reason she felt she was on this earth—even when the rest of the world threw road-blocks in her path.

With their unique gifts, a goal in mind, and faith to bolster their spirits, these fourteen women rose to heights nobody could possibly have imagined. Speaking before millions. Traveling the world. Writing for publication. Setting records in athletics. Starting schools. Marching for their rights and for the rights of others. Performing for kings and queens. Even becoming a friend to a US president. And always paving the way for the next woman.

Why is it so important to read about these remarkable women from long ago? Because they inspire us to think larger and broader than we ordinarily would about our own lives. They inspire us to wonder why we are here and to find out what God has in mind for us to do. And they inspire us to think beyond ourselves to the larger world.

You will read about terrible things done to some of these women—the worst kinds of physical violence, verbal abuse, emotional abuse, and discrimination. But here's the thing they all had in common: they would not hate. Eventually each woman forgave the person, the people, the society—whatever burdened her. Then she moved on to do what she could to repair the world around her.

While each woman forgave, did she also forget? Not exactly—because she knew there must be justice. She also knew she had to pave a way for those who followed her, to help the next sister open a door that had been closed. And again, through it all, our fourteen women simply refused to hate. They are powerful examples for us all.

When I was in Sunday school, I often was told, "Remember, you are the only Bible some people will ever read." That's how these women lived. Most of them were not workers for a church—some could not even read—but each woman lived her faith. To those around her, she often exemplified a life guided by the love of Christ.

You will see in their stories that I refer to these great women by their first names. But if I were standing before them today, I would not speak to them by their first names—it would not be appropriate. I would address each woman as Miss, Mrs., Doctor—whichever title applies—followed by her last name. That would show my respect. But since I want to tell you their stories from childhood on, I chose to use their first names.

One more thing to keep in mind: thanks to the internet, we live in a world where it's easy to access information. We need to remember, however, that while the internet is handy, its information is not always accurate. And the farther back in history we go, the harder it is to get facts. Sometimes I had to choose between conflicting details about a woman's life. So I chose what seemed to make the most sense or what revealed the clearest truth.

I have enjoyed getting to know these fourteen women. It was a privilege to read and write about them. Now I'm eager to introduce you, the reader, to each one . . .

Tricia Williams Jackson

1

Phillis Wheatley

(1753–1784)

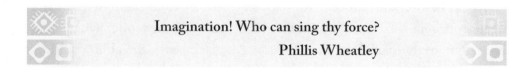

Imagination! Who can sing thy force?
Phillis Wheatley

On a chilly, overcast morning in 1761, the Boston slave market buzzed with activity. White Bostonians crowded around a stage to participate in something all too common in colonial America. They gathered to purchase human beings straight off the boats from Africa to become their personal slaves or to resell them to other white people for slaves.

Several dozen black Africans, including children, stood in a line across the stage and shivered in the damp bay air. Their ankles were chained together. Even the children wore special chains to fit their small ankles. Exhausted and filthy from the long ocean trip, these people had barely survived crossing the Atlantic Ocean. They had been chained in the belly of a slave ship called *The Phillis*. Some of their shipmates had not survived. All of that had been horrible enough. But what was going to happen next?

A thin child from the country of Senegal stood barefoot on the stage. Her ankle chains rubbed her skin. After so long at sea, she felt wobbly standing on land, but she held her ground. She wore a dirty, frayed dress too big for her and a headscarf that once had been brightly colored; now it was dirty from the journey.

The child spoke no English, so she didn't understand a thing the throngs of people around her said. Everything was new and frightening—the shouting of the strangely clothed white men moving swiftly around her, the noisy jostling of the huge horses, the buildings taller than any she'd ever seen. She was shaken by the way the men milling about looked at her and sized her up for purchase, the same way her mother back home might size up chickens at the open-air market. She was even more shaken by the despair on the faces of her adult African shipmates standing with her on the auction block. The child looked around in silent panic.

Weeks before, she had been kidnapped from her village and her family in western Africa, torn from the only home she knew at the tender age of eight. Now, here in the New World, in Boston, Massachusetts, the child could not communicate anything to the people in charge—not her name, not the name of her village, nothing at all. She felt helpless and afraid.

Suddenly, all eyes were on her. She froze as a big man stood behind her, placed his hand on the top of her head, and shouted at the crowd. Men in the crowd called back and forth to the man, and after a time, the man behind her stepped to the side and began shouting again. All eyes moved off the child to the next person in line on the slave block.

By the time the long, confusing day was over, the little Senegalese girl was so tired she could hardly stand. Her chains were removed and left behind. Then she found herself tucked into a horse-drawn carriage and en route to what was to be her new home. She had been purchased by a white man by the name of Mr. John Wheatley, and he and his driver hurried them through the streets as the sun went down.

The carriage stopped at a very large house with many windows, and the child was led inside. The woman of the house, Susanna Wheatley, was powdery white and wearing a dress that made swishing noises when she moved. She smiled at the child while speaking with her husband in their strange language, and she seemed kind. Then the child was taken away by a black woman in white people's clothing who also did not speak anything understandable but was kind and gentle. She helped the child into a hot water bath, dried her with a large towel, slipped an oversized white nightgown over her head, then tucked her into the first bed of the child's young life. Once the child adjusted to the softness of the bed, she slept long and hard.

The next morning, the little girl from Senegal was given new clothes and a name: Phillis Wheatley, her first name after the slave ship that had brought her to America's shores and her last name after the man who had purchased her. It was the custom at the time for a slaveholder to give his last name to the enslaved.

That day, as little Phillis looked around her new setting and felt stiff shoes on her feet for the first time in her life, she knew everything for her was changed forever. In her heart, something shut down. From that day on, it would be as if her life before the ocean journey had never happened; she would never recall her original name after this day. In fact, for the rest of her life, she would remember nothing of her beginning years in Senegal except one vivid image: a sunny African morning in which she watched her tall, willowy mother pour water from a jug.

Phillis Wheatley was born in Senegal, probably in 1753, and like so many west coast Africans in that time was kidnapped to be shipped to America and sold. Slavery in America was the horrible trade of selling human beings—even children and babies—to become slaves to white people. Forced from their homes in Africa and onto wooden ships, black people were then chained in the hold for a dangerous, horrific trip across the Atlantic. Many died on the way, and those who survived often arrived sickly from bad food and lack of fresh air. They would never again see their homes, and most of them would never again be free.

Although Phillis survived the journey, her health suffered greatly on the way. A naturally slender child, she was underweight at the time she was sold, and potential buyers probably thought she was ill. So under the circumstances, Phillis fared better than her shipmates by being purchased by John Wheatley, a wealthy Boston merchant in these days of British rule of the colonies. He purchased her to be a personal maid to his wife, which meant the child would be indoors, well fed, and not forced to work in the fields.

But things turned out even better than that for the little girl. Mrs. Wheatley could see right away that the child was exhausted and ill, so she immediately set to nursing her back to health. And when Susanna Wheatley looked into the child's eyes, she was immediately drawn to her soul. She did not see a slave; she saw a young, intelligent human being.

In spite of the initial language barrier, Susanna Wheatley became aware that this child was quite brilliant. In a time when slaves were never educated—in fact, educating them would become illegal—little Phillis quickly learned to speak proper English, and then she learned to read and write.

John and Susanna Wheatley had eighteen-year-old twins at the time of Phillis's arrival, Mary and Nathaniel, who were also charmed by the thin little African girl. It was Mary who first started teaching Phillis reading and writing, with some help from Nathaniel. Then mother Susanna stepped in and took over, teaching the child as fast as she could learn. The Wheatleys enjoyed teaching this bright child, and the fact that she was a black African child probably made the endeavor more interesting to the family.

This kind of treatment was highly unusual in those times, but John and Susanna decided that nobody would tell them how to handle their household. They certainly believed in slavery; they had many slaves working as servants.

Creation smiles in
various beauty gay

While day to night, and
night succeeds day.

—Phillis Wheatley

But Phillis did not work. She never did become a maid for Mrs. Wheatley. She became more like an adopted family member. She had her own room in the Wheatley mansion, dined at the family table, and was not required to do any work in the house. She attended church with the Wheatleys at the Old South Meeting House in Boston. She accepted Christ into her heart and was baptized in the Old South Meeting House in 1771.

As Phillis grew, she was almost always with white people. In an apparent desire to keep Phillis somehow different from other black people, the Wheatleys did not want her to associate with other slave children. So Phillis did not have many playmates, with one exception. Phillis developed a relationship with one little friend also from Africa named Obour Tanner. Obour had also been purchased by a family who treated her kindly, though they were not as accepting as the Wheatleys. Around Boston, Phillis would be referred to by others as a Wheatley "servant," but this was more polite than true; by law, Phillis was still a slave.

By the time she was age twelve (and some sources say age nine), Phillis was most likely the best educated female in Boston—even more educated than the Wheatley women. Phillis not only studied classic literature, geology, history, astronomy, and the Bible, but she could read Greek and Latin. She was so bright that the family liked to show her off to visitors. Most colonists didn't believe a nonwhite person, much less a female, could be so intellectually accomplished. But seeing was believing. When Phillis began writing poetry, eventually even getting it published, Bostonians were more amazed.

Phillis Wheatley loved writing poetry. It soothed her sensitive spirit, and she found a thrill in developing a beautiful, musical piece of structured writing—that is, a poem. When she was twelve, her first poem was published in the newspaper *Newport Mercury*. She wrote poems with Christian themes and ideas, and she also liked writing elegies, which are often poems written to honor the dead. She seldom wrote about herself, though she wrote eloquently about her observations and beliefs.

Her best-known poem is one she wrote in 1770 about coming to America to be enslaved and what that ultimately meant to her.

On Being Brought from Africa to America

'Twas mercy brought me from my Pagan land,
Taught my benighted soul to understand
That there's a God, that there's a Saviour too:
Once I redemption neither sought nor knew.
Some view our sable race with scornful eye,
"Their colour is a diabolic die."
Remember, Christians, Negros, black as Cain,
May be refin'd and join th'angelic train.

In this poem, Phillis expresses herself in the manner people wrote in those days by using formal language and rhymed lines. The poem talks about her Christianity and her gratitude for it. She calls it a "mercy" that she was kidnapped from her "Pagan land" because it led her to her faith. Some modern readers today find the poem offensive, as if Phillis were making slavery somehow good. But it's best to take it as she meant it—that through Christ a great good can come out of a horrible bad.

Besides, in her lifetime Phillis would write plenty against slavery. Even in this poem, she says: "Some view our sable race with scornful eye." This is where Phillis gently scolds racist readers who believed black people could not be Christians—a common belief of the day when many white people saw black people as not fully human and not even possessing a soul. Regardless of any controversy, readers realized it was a masterful poem.

Phillis eventually challenged herself by writing poetry about the events of the day. These were the years colonists lived in America before the Revolutionary War. When war issues became more heated, Phillis wrote a poem praising King George III of England. But as the revolutionary energy in New England grew stronger, she found things at home to write about. In the days just before the American Revolution, there was plenty going on in Boston!

News of this fine young poet spread around New England. Then, in 1772, young Phillis was taken in front of a committee of eighteen male judges to discuss her poetry and to determine if they should publish a book of her poems. The men were very impressed with the poetry, but they could not believe such writing could come from a woman or a black person, much less both in one young person. They simply did not believe she wrote her poems. So they did not publish them.

Nevertheless Susanna Wheatley continued to encourage young Phillis in her poetry writing. Susanna made sure Phillis had plenty of paper and ink for her quill pen. Often she took Phillis out to meet influential people of the times, including Ben Franklin.

Phillis and the Wheatleys' son Nathaniel traveled to England. Since her landing in Boston, Phillis had always been frail, suffering chronically from an ailment that was either asthma or tuberculosis. The Wheatley family doctor suggested she take this trip for her health. Given the danger and discomfort of sea voyages then, one might wonder why he would suggest such a thing. But in those days, salt sea air was seen as truly beneficial to one's heath, especially if one were, as they said then, "delicate." Phillis was delicate indeed. A change of scenery was also seen as helpful for the sickly.

So she prepared to take the long journey with both joy and trepidation. She had always wanted to meet England's King George, the subject of one of her poems. She mostly wanted to see if her poems might be published in England since the American publishing judges did not believe she wrote them.

But it was the first time she had left the shores of America since she had arrived in chains. Her mind did not remember much about that horrible sea journey from Africa, in which she was chained in the hold while all around her people were sick and dying. But she was anxious. What if something happened to the Wheatleys while she was away? It was hard not to worry about the only family, of sorts, that she had. Regardless of her fears, Phillis boarded the ship and made the journey safely to London, England, with Nathaniel Wheatley looking out for her.

Londoners immediately took to this bright and slender young woman, and Phillis was pleasantly surprised by this. She wrote back home that she was pleased with "the unexpected and unmerited civility and complaisance with which I was treated by all." In other words, the people of England liked her very much and treated her with genuine hospitality.

As the year turned over into 1773, Phillis found her success. Her first and only book of poems was published in England. It was the first book ever to be written by a black American woman. Titled *Poems on Various Subjects, Religious and Moral*, the book of thirty-nine poems brought Phillis literary fame in England.

By 1774 her book arrived in America to be sold there, and it was advertised immediately. The books sold out and more had to be ordered from England. Phillis was thrilled, and so were the Wheatleys. It was a dream come true.

Susanna Wheatley, who by now considered herself Phillis's adopted mother, took ill that spring, and Phillis hurried back to America to assist her. But Susanna died soon after Phillis's arrival. Before she passed away, she expressed how proud she was that she lived long enough to see Phillis's book published. Devastated by Susanna's death, Phillis funneled her grief into her poetry.

The American Revolution was in full swing by now, and Phillis became a fan of George Washington. In 1776 she wrote him a letter of support and included a poem she had written called "To His Excellency General Washington." Washington was impressed. He called Phillis a "poetical genius," and he invited her to visit him, saying that he would be "happy to see a person so favored by the muses."

In Washington's reply to the poet, he referred to her as "Miss Phillis." This was a surprising show of respect for a black person at the time. They were never referred to as Mr., Mrs., or Miss by a white person. Phillis traveled to meet George Washington, and they met and talked for about half an hour. They remained long-distance fans of one another.

In 1778, only a few years after Susanna died, John Wheatley also died. Very soon after, Mary Wheatley died too. Each death was a great personal loss for Phillis. She also lost her way of life. She had been the member of a wealthy household and had lived an unusually privileged life. Now that household and that life were gone.

Phillis was shaken to the core, living without the people who had literally taken care of her. John's will left Phillis a legally free woman, but she was also left to support herself, something she had never done in her life. In all of her years in America, Phillis had been treated mostly the same as a wealthy white female. Writing paid a little but not often or enough. She did find work as a seamstress, since even fine ladies were taught to use needle and thread. But she was simply unable to make a living sewing clothing for others.

This trouble in earning a living is probably why, three months after Mary's death, Phillis married. Her husband was a free black man named John Peters. He was in business for himself as a grocer, but not successfully, and the two lived in poverty. John Peters also had debt, which was considered a serious legal offense then.

Probably due to Phillis's delicate health, their first two children both died soon after they were born. After the birth of their third child, John was taken away to debtors' prison. Now Phillis was alone with an infant to care for. She and her baby lived in a tiny room in a boardinghouse. Phillis was unable to find publishers to buy her writing anymore, so now she worked off her rent as a maid at the boardinghouse. Nothing in her background at the Wheatley home had prepared her for this life. And her health continued to go downhill.

Life was not kind to Phillis in the end. Poverty, grief, and the aftereffects of childbirth worsened her chronic health problems. In 1784, at age thirty-one, she died in her room in the boardinghouse. A few hours later, her baby died too. Phillis and her baby were buried together in an unmarked grave somewhere in Boston, Massachusetts.

While those final years of Phillis's life were sad ones, today we remember Phillis Wheatley as a fine poet in the early years of our nation. She had many "firsts." She was our first African-American poet. She was the first African-American woman and the first slave to have a published book. And she was the first African American to earn money with her writing. In her life, she wrote over a hundred poems, the last one about George Washington. Some of her poems are forever lost, but many of them were collected after her death, thanks to her husband and some Boston literary collectors.

A lovely bronze statue of the brilliant and elegant Phillis Wheatley can be seen at the Boston Women's Memorial. Her face is serious, her expression thoughtful. It's as if she's composing a poem. Or maybe she's thanking God for the gift of imagination—a gift that could help a spirit soar no matter what.

◉ Think…

1. What one childhood memory did Phillis Wheatley have of her life in Africa?

2. Phillis came to America before it was officially a nation. When was the American Revolution?

3. Why was Phillis Wheatley's book of poems published in England rather than in Boston?

◈ Imagine…

Young Phillis had her own room in the Wheatley house in Boston. Think about what that room looked like. How many windows? How many books? Can you name any titles?

◉ Get Creative!

Use pencils or markers to illustrate one of Phillis's windows. What is framed in that window? What is in the sky? What did Boston look like then?

2

Sojourner Truth

(1797–1883)

 I feel safe in the midst of my enemies, for the truth is all powerful and will prevail.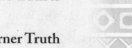

Sojourner Truth

The little girl and her smaller brother watched their mother, whom everyone called Mau Mau, rock back and forth, back and forth. Her sad brown eyes were moist with unshed tears. Once in a while she'd shake her head and wipe her eyes. And rock some more.

The children were the two youngest of their mother's ten or twelve children. The little girl never knew for certain how many siblings she had, since all the previous children had been taken by the plantation owner and sold, never to be seen again. The last two little children—sold before the little girl was born—were the two who had finally broken their mother's heart completely. She never got over losing them.

Mau Mau told of it often. It had been a snowy New York winter, and the master brought a handsome, horse-drawn sleigh by the slave quarters. Mau Mau's five-year-old boy, a cheery little child by nature, became so excited to see that sleigh that he climbed right on board, laughing. Only then did he see that his two-year-old sister had already been secretly grabbed and put into a wooden box on the sleigh.

The boy jumped down and ran back to his mother in panic. But a white man grabbed him and put him back in the sleigh, which quickly took off. Mau Mau never saw those children again.

Mau Mau bore two more babies—the little girl and her younger brother— and so far she had been able to keep them from being taken. But she never got over losing her previous two children. She would speak of it often, telling the sad story over and over while rocking back and forth.

Listening to Mau Mau's grieving were the little girl's first memories.

The little girl was named Isabella Baumfree, and that would be her name until the day she would change it. For now, and for much of her life, everyone called her Bell. She was born into slavery in rural New York in 1797, not long after the American Revolution.

In this part of New York, most white people were of Dutch descent and only spoke Dutch, so Dutch was also Bell's first language. Mau Mau was the daughter of slaves from Ghana, Africa. Bell's father had been captured and enslaved in Ghana. He was tall and lean, and he was given his last name by white men based on his appearance. "Baum" means tree in German, but it was also the word these New York Dutch–speaking people used for tree. Why "free" was added nobody knew. In any event, "Baumfree" became Bell's last name as well. Bell would grow to be six feet tall with an erect posture just like her father's.

As a child, Bell lived with her brother and her parents in a cold, dark cellar under a building, along with all the slaves of the farm. They all slept together on straw on the floor—adult, child, male, female. This was in New York State, a place of extreme seasons. Throughout the year, dampness seeped in, then ice, then mud, then summer heat—and the slaves lived with all that on a floor of straw. It was a place where sickness would thrive in filth and bad weather. As Bell's parents got older, they developed ailments that would be worsened from the dampness and the chill.

Childhood was not kind to Bell. She was sold from her family the first time at age nine, along with a flock of sheep. In the following year she learned to speak English, partly to avoid punishment for speaking Dutch. She was whipped often and sometimes severely so—she would carry scars on her back all her life from childhood whippings. She served in several different plantations by the time she was a young adult, eventually landing at a plantation owned by a Mr. Dumont.

When she was a young woman, Bell fell in love with a man named Robert, a slave at a neighboring plantation. Robert's owner did not want him involved with Bell because he didn't own her, so any children they may have together he also would not own. One day, when Robert was visiting Bell while she was sick, Robert's owner was so incensed that he came after him at the Dumont place. On the spot, he beat Robert so savagely he would have killed him had Dumont not stepped in. Bell watched it all in horror.

Bell and Robert never saw each other again after that, and Robert married the woman his master ordered him to marry—one of his own slaves. But Robert's injuries were so excessive that, not long after the beating, he died as a result of them. Bell never forgot about it the rest of her life.

Bell married a man named Thomas whom Dumont wanted her to marry. She had five children with Thomas. Four of the children lived beyond childbirth. With each baby, Bell continued to work in the fields. She would place her baby in a basket, tie the two handles to a secure piece of cloth, and loop that over a tree limb with a sash hanging down. Then an older child would pull the sash to rock the baby in the basket. She worked at Dumont's place and kept her children there for many years. At some point after her fifth child, her husband, Thomas, died.

Dumont promised Bell her freedom in 1826 if she would continue to be a faithful worker. She agreed. But he didn't do what he promised. So Bell stayed for a few more months, then she decided she'd worked for her freedom long enough. She was supposed to be free now, so she was walking away. One day she took her infant daughter and moved to the home of Mr. and Mrs. Van Wagenen, a kind Christian white couple who did not believe in slavery. "I did not run off," Bell would say about taking her leave, "for I thought that wicked, but I walked off, believing that to be all right." Bell lived with the Van Wagenens with her baby Sophia, but she would have to leave the rest of her children behind—son Peter and daughters Diana and Elizabeth—until they reached adulthood.

According to law, Bell's children could not be sold out of state. Yet a couple of years later she learned that her five-year-old son, Peter, had been sold to a man in Alabama. With the help of the Van Wagenens and through a lot of work, Bell did the impossible—she sued in court. A black woman—a former slave— actually took to court the white man who had sold her enslaved son. Against all odds, Bell won her case. She was the first black woman in America to do such a thing: take a white man to court and win. Her son was given back to her.

When little Peter was in the courtroom, however, he seemed frantic and did not recognize his mother. Fortunately the court took Bell's word that he was her son, and after she won her case, Bell talked soothingly to Peter to get him to come around. She fed him candy and assured him she was his mother. He finally said that she looked familiar. Then she learned that Peter was so afraid of his owner that he could not allow himself to acknowledge his mother in the courtroom.

Bell took her son home, and he finally relaxed and knew her. Only then did she discover his little body was covered in welts. He confessed he'd been whipped, kicked, or beaten almost daily.

Where there is so much
racket, there must be
something out of kilter.

—*Sojourner Truth*

This injustice to her small son devastated Bell. The fact that someone had been hurting her child was almost too much to bear. But at least she had him back. Fortunately, in 1827 slavery in New York State ended—many years before it ended in the nation.

While Bell lived with the Van Wagenens, she became a strong Christian. Mau Mau had taught her about God but not a lot—and nothing about Jesus. Bell had seen her Mau Mau pray, and in her child's mind she somehow got the idea that God would do whatever she asked him to do if she prayed for it in time. She didn't ask for much or ask very often, but it turned out that anything she prayed for did happen. That's as much as Bell understood of prayer until she met the Van Wagenens. Now that she knew who Jesus was, and that prayer wasn't simply a wish list but rather a relationship, Bell's spirit soared with her new belief.

On June 1, 1843, Bell changed her name. She told her friends and her children: "The Spirit calls me and I must go." She had decided that she would travel as a preacher of truth and a worker against injustice. From that day on, she would be known as Sojourner Truth. She eventually would join the church denomination of Seventh Day Adventists.

For the next forty years, Sojourner Truth traveled around the northeastern and midwestern United States, preaching about the abolition of slavery and all its cruelties. She also spoke on temperance (the fight against alcohol consumption), and she spoke for women's rights at a time when women simply didn't have any rights. She spoke of love for all people and kindness to those in need.

She was unusual. She was an independent African-American woman who seemed at ease wherever she was and whomever she was with. At six feet tall with a straight spine and long limbs, when she walked into a room people knew it. When she spoke to an audience, her deep, strong voice could be heard. And she was well received, though occasionally she would be booed and hissed by men in the room. On one of those occasions, she responded, "You may hiss as much as you please, but women will get their rights anyway. You can't stop us, neither."

Sojourner had friends who suggested she publish her personal story for all to read. So she dictated the story of her life and her faith to a friend, and in 1850 another friend published her book, *The Narrative of Sojourner Truth: A Northern Slave.* This fascinating memoir is still available to read online today. She sold the book when she traveled and spoke, and she also sold cards with a photograph of herself and a line underneath that said, "I sell the shadow to support the substance." This most likely simply meant she was selling a photo of herself to feed herself.

Many people today know Sojourner Truth as a woman who gave a famous speech eventually known as "Ain't I a Woman?" This took place at the Women's Convention in Akron, Ohio, in 1851. The speech, which Sojourner gave in response to some things a man said about the inferior nature of women, has over time gone through many revisions. Since Sojourner could not read, she did not write her speech down, but others took notes. The following is most likely closest to the speech she actually gave, as reported by newspaper editor Marius Robinson. This is the version published in newspapers at the time:

I want to say a few words about this matter. I am a woman's rights. [*sic*] I have as much muscle as any man, and can do as much work as any man. I have plowed and reaped and husked and chopped and mowed, and can any man do more than that? I have heard much about the sexes being equal. I can carry as much as any man, and can eat as much too, if I can get it. I am as strong as any man that is now. As for intellect, all I can say is, if a woman have a pint, and a man a quart—why can't she have her little pint full? You need not be afraid to give us our rights for fear we will take too much,—for we can't take more than our pint'll hold. The poor men seems to be all in confusion, and don't know what to do. Why children, if you have woman's rights, give it to her and you will feel better. You will have your own rights, and they won't be so much trouble. I can't read, but I can hear. I have heard the Bible and have learned that Eve caused man to sin. Well, if woman upset the world, do give her a chance to set it right side up again. The Lady has spoken about Jesus, how he never spurned woman from him, and she was right. When Lazarus died, Mary and Martha came to him with faith and love and besought him to raise their brother. And Jesus wept and Lazarus came forth. And how came Jesus into the world? Through God who created him and the woman who bore him. Man, where was your part? But the women are coming up, blessed be God, and a few of the men are coming up with them. But man is in a tight place, the poor slave is on him, woman is coming on him, he is surely between a hawk and a buzzard.

For someone who could neither read nor write, Sojourner Truth was clearly masterful at painting pictures with words and weaving in the Scripture she had heard read and had memorized. Noting at the end that men were now "between a hawk and a buzzard" was her more creative way of saying what

Let others say what they will
of the efficacy of prayer;
I believe in it, and I shall pray.
Thank God! Yes, I shall always pray.

—*Sojourner Truth*

people often say today to describe a tough situation—"between a rock and a hard place." In the speech's case, she's saying men had lots of rights to share with their fellow Americans, including both slaves (they had not yet been freed) and women.

But twelve years later, during the Civil War, Frances Dana Barker Gage "remembered" the speech differently. Now a revised version was published in newspapers so many years after the fact.

Sometimes ethnic groups and slaves might speak English in their own unique way or dialect, and Gage presented Sojourner's speech in a manner that would suggest she was speaking with a Southern accent and no grammar skills. It's called writing in dialect, something we usually avoid doing today regarding someone's manner of speech. But it's worth noting how it was written then. Here is only one paragraph, written as Gage claimed Sojourner Truth said it:

Dat man ober dar say dat womin needs to be helped into carriages, and lifted ober ditches, and to hab de best place everywhar. Nobody ever helps me into carriages, or ober mud-puddles, or gibs me any best place! And ain't I a woman? Look at me! Look at my arm! I have ploughed, and planted, and gathered into barns, and no man could head me! And ain't I a woman? I could work as much and eat as much as a man—when I could get it—and bear de lash as well! And ain't I a woman? I have borne thirteen chilern, and seen 'em mos' all sold off to slavery, and when I cried out with my mother's grief, none but Jesus heard me! And ain't I a woman?

That is the version people read today. This is odd for many reasons. First of all, Sojourner Truth was not Southern. She was Northern, and she didn't speak with a Southern accent. Her first language was Dutch, so while it's possible she had a slight Germanic-sounding accent, it's not likely—she learned English at age nine. She took pride in speaking good, clear, and mostly grammatical English. She certainly would not have been invited to give speeches to the public if she had been hard to understand. Also she gave birth to five children, not thirteen as this speech claims. This "Ain't I a Woman?" speech is these days considered by experts to be a misrepresentation of what she actually said on this occasion. Nevertheless, that's the version history books tend to report.

But no matter which speech one reads, Sojourner Truth's point is clear. She cautions men not to make such sweeping judgments on the abilities of women or underestimate the intelligence of women or think women weak. They would simply be wrong to do that, and she offers herself as all the evidence she needs.

In 1864, while the Civil War still raged, Sojourner made a visit to the White House to meet President Abraham Lincoln. It was a little over a week prior to election day, when the nation would elect Lincoln to his second term as president. Exactly how this meeting came about is unknown. But the meeting was described as simply two people who fought for freedom meeting on equal ground as abolitionists. Sojourner praised the president and offered her views on the state of the nation. The president told Sojourner that he knew of her work as an abolitionist and held tremendous respect for her. A famous illustration exists that depicts this meeting. In this drawing, Sojourner sits with an open Bible before her, and the president stands next to her. The dignity of both individuals is clear to see.

Sojourner Truth spent the rest of her life moving from place to place, meeting people, preaching to those who would listen. She eventually moved to Battle Creek, Michigan, where there was a large and active community of Seventh Day Adventists, and she made that city her final residence. She continued to travel widely, speaking at churches and conventions not only about slavery and women's rights but now also about prison reform and capital punishment. She became friends with important people and common people both, and she earned the respect of such notable women as women's rights activist Susan B. Anthony and Quaker Lucretia Mott.

Sojourner died in her Battle Creek home in 1883 at age eighty-six. She had lived to see slavery end, but she did not live to see women get the right to vote. Her funeral was held at the Battle Creek Tabernacle where, some reports claim, three thousand people, black and white, crowded in to pay their respects. She was buried without a marker until, years later, a collection was taken in Battle Creek to purchase and erect a very handsome cemetery monument for her.

Sojourner Truth was a rare American woman. She was a former slave who had unusually hopeful and forward thinking. She lived with so much evil and unkindness directed at her that she easily could have become hateful. But she did not. She let the light of Christ pull her up so that she could speak truth and help other people.

She worked for the benefit of others for much of her long, extraordinary life. Those who knew her personally were fortunate—and thankfully, they made certain that future generations could know her too.

● Think…

1. Sojourner Truth's first memories were watching her mother rock and cry. Why was her mother so distressed?

2. What was Sojourner's first language? When and why did she learn to speak English?

3. When Sojourner said to her friends, "The Spirit calls me and I must go," what did she do then?

◆ Imagine…

If you were going to change your name, what would you call yourself? Why?

■ Get Creative!

Draw a map of Sojourner's wanderings around parts of America. Start where she was born. End where she died. Illustrate the map at spots where she stopped or lived.

3

Harriet Tubman

(1822–1913)

 Every great dream begins with a dreamer.
Harriet Tubman

In a pine forest near a saltwater marsh in Maryland in the early 1800s, a young girl stood still, her hand resting on a tree. She cocked her head and listened. It was Sunday, so some of the slaves at the plantation did not need to work, including her and her parents. So she and her father were in the woods looking for greens for Mama to boil for supper. But they were also playing a game. Could the little girl come up behind her father without him knowing it?

It was hard to do. Papa could hunt rabbits without a gun, and he knew how to stay stone still and listen to the sounds in the forest. Many times when they went searching for greens, Papa would say, "Child, listen to that sound—when you hear that sound, there's another person out here. . . . Do you see him?" The girl would listen and look until she finally saw that someone else was also searching for greens many yards away, mostly hidden by the dense trees.

"Do you think you could sneak up behind your old papa and not have him hear you? Try it." And she would try, but it seemed like she always did something like break a branch or trip on a cluster of weeds. Papa would hear it and look right at her and shake his head and grin. Then they'd look for supper greens.

While searching for greens, he would also instruct her on the ways of the forest. "See those willow trees? That means there's water nearby." And "See this moss on the bark? That faces north. You can always feel it on the tree even if you can't see it." He showed her how to predict the next day's weather by looking at the sky and smelling the air. He showed her edible things growing in the forest. Sometimes, at night, Papa took her outside to explain the constellations of stars and to teach her to find the North Star. "That way you always know where you are," he said. The child learned to be as comfortable in nature as her father was.

Today the child was especially stealthy. She watched her father from behind a stand of trees. She stayed perfectly still, knowing she had positioned herself to blend in with the piney bark. She moved from tree to tree when Papa looked the other way, until eventually she crept behind him and tapped him on the shoulder.

Papa jumped and turned in one move, then grinned from ear to ear. He nodded. "You got it, child, you got it."

It would be a few more years before she would realize exactly why Papa had taught her the ways of the woods and the night sky.

Harriet Tubman was named Araminta Ross when she was born, and she was nicknamed Minty. She was the youngest of ten children of Ben and Harriet

Ross, slaves on the Brodas Plantation. The parents loved and enjoyed this youngest child, but always feared losing her. They had already lost two of their daughters—sold off to a chain gang as small children and never seen again. Mama prayed daily that this would not happen to any of her other children.

Mama and Papa Ross taught little Minty about God and how to pray. They sang spirituals to her, and she enjoyed singing back to them, songs like "Go Down, Moses" and "Oh, Mary Don't You Weep."

But when Minty was six, she was sold, put into a wagon, and taken away. She'd never set foot off the Brodas Plantation in her life. She'd never spent a night away from Mama. As the wagon rolled away, little Minty was so frightened she could hardly move. Her destination was a small farm, where she was to work inside the family's log house.

Even though the house was small, it was far bigger than Minty was used to. She and the members of her family still at home had all slept in a tiny one-room cabin by the light of a fire. They had kept each other warm on cold nights. It never occurred to Minty that it was crowded. It was cozy and it was home.

Now she would sleep alone in front of another fireplace. Sleeping on the floor there was a cold experience. She was fed very little food and was always hungry. She was expected to help the lady who lived there with her wool spinning. But so much contact with the fiber and lint caused little Minty what was probably an allergic reaction to it. She could not stop sneezing.

She was then sent outside to work with the husband, who hunted and trapped animals for their fur. Minty was in charge of watching a line of muskrat traps in the river. When a muskrat was caught in the trap, she hauled it up. The trap and the animal together weighed probably a third of Minty's own weight, and the work was hard for a little girl. And it was cold at a time when she only wore a cotton shift and worked in her bare feet. But Minty would rather be in the outdoors than in that horrid house of lint.

Overwork, exposure to the damp cold, and very little nutrition eventually caused Minty to get sick. She came down with the measles and a fever, then she developed bronchitis. The trapper and his wife wrapped her up in a blanket and simply left her alone. They hoped she would heal. They had, after all, paid money for her.

Word somehow got back to the Brodas Plantation of Minty's serious illness, and her mother was able to talk Mr. Brodas into taking Minty back so her mother could nurse her back to health. Once Minty was back in their cabin, Mama used healing herbs and nutritious food to make her better.

When she recovered, Minty was sent back to the log cabin. This time she had to work indoors and learn to weave, something she would never be any good at. But in the end, she was sold back to Mr. Brodas. The trapper couple told him Minty was too "stupid and lazy" to work, and they didn't want her anymore.

Back in her mama's care, little Minty slept and slept. When she was awake, Mama gave her food and herbs. The bronchitis had altered Minty's voice, and now a deep, almost male-sounding voice came out of that little body. Her voice would be deep and distinct for the rest of her life.

Now the Rosses were worried that their little girl might be seen as a problem, and that could cause her to be sold to a chain gang. This was a constant worry for all slaves, that loved ones—spouses and children—would be sold away from them. If a chain gang came through and the master of the plantation needed cash, all slaves were vulnerable to being sold on the spot.

So, by comparison, it was better than it could have been when Minty was sold to a neighboring plantation to work indoors. But this did not go well. Minty was a small child raised in a cabin with a dirt floor and no possessions. What did she know about cleaning house and dusting and caring for a baby? The mistress of the house was constantly impatient with Minty and whipped her often. The day came when Minty could not take the whippings and ran away. But she had no idea where she was, so she came back.

Now Minty was whipped worse than ever. Then the couple loaded the bleeding, unconscious child into a wagon and returned her to Mr. Brodas, saying they wanted their money back because Minty was a useless worker.

I freed a thousand slaves.
I could have freed a thousand more
if only they knew they were slaves.

—Harriet Tubman

Once again Mama nursed her child back to health, but now she also tended to the deep welts on her baby girl's back. Mama spent hours praying over Minty and sponging healing teas onto the welts from that awful whipping.

Mr. Brodas waited for Minty to get better. Then he assured her parents he would not sell her again. Instead he would "hire her out." This is when the slaveholder would be paid by outside people for use of his slaves. So that's what happened.

As time went on and Minty reached twelve years old, she also reached her full height of five feet. She had become a lean and muscular young woman who did a man's work on a regular basis. As a young adult, she now wore a dress and covered her head with a wrapped bandana in the style of other grown black women around her. When necessary, she had a way of tucking her skirt's hem into her waistband so that she wore something like trousers. She worked in the fields alongside other slaves.

One day, a fellow fieldworker noted that another slave was missing. The man whispered that the slave had taken the "Underground Railroad" and wouldn't be back.

What does he mean? Minty wondered. *Did the man get on a train?* By careful and quiet asking, Minty eventually learned that the Underground Railroad was a system of quietly moving escaped slaves from place to place, ultimately to the North and to freedom. It was top secret and only discussed in whispers. And it was very dangerous. First you had to trust the white people who were involved. And you absolutely could not get caught. Getting caught in an escape would be much worse than living daily as a slave. Minty knew this was true; she well remembered that final whipping. She tucked this Underground Railroad information into the back of her mind and went about her work.

One day several workers were working together near the outbuildings and being watched by an overseer. Minty noticed one of the workers acting oddly. When the overseer turned his back, suddenly the slave took off running. Nobody said anything, so he was halfway across a field before the overseer noticed and took off after him. Without thinking, only acting on instinct, Minty took off after the overseer.

The three caught up with each other in another barn. The overseer had the slave cornered, and when he saw Minty he ordered her to tie the man up so he could be whipped. Instead, Minty stood and looked at both men, back and forth. The slave saw his opportunity in this hesitation and took off again for the door.

The overseer started to follow, but Minty stood in his path. When he tried to get around her, young Minty continued to block him. The overseer grabbed a two-pound brick and threw it at the runaway, but his aim fell short. The brick hit Minty square in the middle of her forehead and knocked her out.

This injury almost killed Minty. She lay unconscious for months, and even when she did start to wake up, she would fall back asleep while sitting. It was the love and care of her mother that brought her back to health. Mama nursed her head wound and prayed over her.

Fellow slaves at the Brodas Plantation were amazed by and proud of this young woman who had literally risked her life for the sake of a runaway slave. What honor could they bestow on Minty under the circumstances? They had nothing. And it would need to be quiet. So they determined not to call Minty by her baby name anymore. The slave community showed their respect for Araminta Ross by renaming her after her mother—Harriet—and she was Harriet from that day on.

With such a bad head injury, once young Harriet could stay awake she still needed to learn to speak and walk again. It took a long time. She could never be sold because word of her actions had gone out. Plus, she had a huge scar on her forehead for the rest of her life, and that scar made some people nervous when they looked at it. She had horrible headaches now, bad enough that she would be unable to do anything until they faded away. Worse than that, now she had occasional episodes where she would suddenly pass out and collapse. She would stay in a deep sleep for up to several hours, then wake up as if nothing had happened. But while unconscious, she had vivid visions she recalled upon waking up. It was unnerving.

All this meant Mr. Brodas could not sell or hire out this young slave. And that made life dangerous for Harriet. She used to pray for Mr. Brodas, that he would not sell her away. But as Harriet healed, she found a burning anger growing inside her. She began to call on God to kill Mr. Brodas. She actually prayed that this would happen. She prayed passionately and constantly to God: *Kill him, Lord. Kill him.*

And a few days after Harriet began praying for the death of Mr. Brodas, he did indeed die.

Harriet was horrified. She begged God's forgiveness for what she had prayed, and she never again prayed for a bad thing to happen to anyone. It would take her awhile to understand that she had not caused Mr. Brodas's death. Mr. Brodas had simply died. But Harriet determined that she would use whatever she could to do God's will, not her own, in this world.

As Harriet regained her strength, she was able to work in the fields again. The new owner of the plantation agreed to hire her out. This also allowed her to live with her parents. Papa picked right up where he left off in teaching his baby girl how to listen to the natural world. Harriet learned much from him in terms of how noisy a forest could be and what that meant, how to read the sky, what birdcalls meant. Then he began teaching her the geography of the area, locations of rivers and nearby towns. She would need this information one day.

Eventually Harriet fell in love with a handsome man named John Tubman. He had gained his freedom and now worked for his own money. They decided to marry. Of course, slaves actually had no legal right to do anything, much less marry. Often they were simply fixed up with another slave and told to be a couple—and one or the other could be sold away at any time.

Luckier slaves had owners who would allow them to take as a husband or wife someone of their own choosing. There was no religious service; a couple might jump over a broom together to show they were married. That's all they were allowed. But they took that vow more seriously than did their masters who felt free to break up marriages and families anytime cash was low.

In 1844 Harriet and John made the commitment to each other that was as close to a legal marriage as they could have. Harriet left her parents' cabin and moved in with her husband.

By the following year, there was more quiet chatter in the fields about escaped slaves making it to freedom via the Underground Railroad. One day Harriet spoke to John about it. "We could get on that Railroad," she said, "and be free together. Then nobody could separate us."

But John surprised Harriet by getting angry. He didn't want to go north. He felt he was making enough money to give them a pretty good life, all things considered. He didn't seem to care that Harriet wasn't free. In fact, it was worse than that—he told Harriet that if she tried to escape, he'd tell her master.

This was shocking. Harriet's own husband, threatening to betray her to the man who legally owned her? "You don't care that we could be separated forever if the master sold me away?" she said in disbelief. "You don't care that whatever children we have wouldn't be free?"

John glared at her and said again, "You try to escape, I will tell."

Now Harriet had to see her husband differently. Now she was afraid of him. During the next few years, Harriet thought often about escaping to freedom. She truly believed God wanted her free, but she kept these thoughts from John.

It was three years before Harriet decided to make a run for it. She had been having nightmares every night about being sold. Then, one of those nights, she also dreamed she was swimming across a river. She began to drown, but some women dressed in white grabbed her hands and pulled her across. When she woke up, she knew from the earlier dreams that she was in trouble. She thought the women in white were angels, and she decided this was God's way of telling her she would be successful if she tried to escape. She waited for the right time to flee.

One day, while she was working the fields, a white woman wearing a black dress and white cap and driving a horse-drawn wagon stopped next to where Harriet was working. The two had a conversation, Harriet's first with a white person who treated her like an equal. The woman, Harriet would learn, was a Quaker. After the woman had stopped by a few times, she told Harriet where she lived and added, "If thee ever needs anything—anything at all—come by."

That day came in 1849. Harriet heard in the fields that she was about to be sold to the chain gang. That simply could not happen. Harriet thought it over and wondered if the women in white in her dream meant she would be helped by a white woman. She decided, yes, it all made sense.

That night, after John fell asleep, Harriet took a bandana and filled it with food and a few possessions and headed quietly outside. She walked through the slave quarters to the Big House where her sister worked as a cook. Harriet composed a song on the spot outside the kitchen and sang in her distinctive voice, hoping her sister would hear and understand: "Good-bye, I'm going to leave you. . . . Good-bye, I'll meet you in the Kingdom . . ."

Harriet walked away from everything she had ever known and the only man she would ever love. With an encouraging song in her head, she walked to the Quaker woman's house.

The Quaker woman was indeed helpful. She gave Harriet a piece of paper with some writing on it, directed her to the next stop, and told her to show that paper to the people at that next stop. For the next several days, Harriet was at the mercy of strangers, most of them white and some of them black, who fed her and sheltered her and spirited her away, sometimes by wagon, sometimes by boat, sometimes by horse, and always at night. It was all quite miraculous. Harriet knew God had blessed her journey.

Eventually, Harriet was free and in the city of Philadelphia, Pennsylvania. There she worked several jobs to put money away in hopes of getting her family members north. She met other escaped former slaves, and she started to understand the system of the Underground Railroad. In fact, the day came when she felt she understood it so well that she decided to sneak back south and see if she could bring any family members or anyone else back north with her.

Escaping was one thing. Going back was another. She would be easier to catch, and if she were caught she would be severely punished, maybe killed. But Harriet understood fully what she was doing. She understood the escape system, and thanks to her papa she understood the geography of escaping from her former home. More importantly, however, Harriet felt freedom was solidly in God's will, and even if she lost her life, helping slaves to freedom was her destiny.

Over the next several years, Harriet would show up in her old slave quarters at night. She would walk through and sing songs to let people know she was there and would escort them north. Slaves would hear that deep voice singing:

> I am bound for the freedom land,
> I am bound for the freedom land.

O who will come and go with me?
I am bound for the freedom land.

Those who were ready would go. They called her Moses, and they literally put their lives in Harriet's hands to lead them over dangerous territory at tremendous risk.

Not only was the journey itself difficult, but Harriet did worry about her sleeping fits. One time, in the middle of the road in broad daylight, she sank to the road and fell sound asleep. The several slaves she had with her had heard about these sleeping fits. They all sat on the ground around her and waited for two hours until she woke up.

When Harriet awakened, she was startled and agitated. Everyone was in the road in broad daylight! She hurried them off the road and explained that she'd had a vivid vision that they needed to go in the opposite direction they'd been traveling and head for a river. She'd seen it all plotted out in her vision. She insisted everyone stay silent and follow her.

Harriet took her charges back through the woods they'd just gone through, silently zigzagging their way to the river. At the river, she got everyone across to the other side. Wet and chilled, they continued on a bit, then stopped to rest. Now they could hear hound dogs baying back where they came from. Had they continued north when Harriet awakened, they would have been caught. Zigzagging in the forest meant the hounds chasing them were slowed, and crossing the river meant the dogs lost their scent. The group made it north to safety.

Harriet went back home to take dozens more people out of the area. Eventually there was a huge bounty on Harriet's head. Anyone who captured her could be awarded thousands of dollars, which today would be more like millions. Harriet literally laughed it off. She would not worry about such things; God was in control of this mission.

One of the more daring trips Harriet made involved her parents. She'd had vivid dreams they were going to be separated and sold. She learned that Papa was being watched for feeding a runaway and was potentially in trouble. She hurried south and made it to their cabin one night. She told them she was there to take them north.

But both the Rosses were old and had arthritis pain. Taking them north on foot was impossible. They knew what Harriet did, and they were proud of her, but they also knew they couldn't make the trip.

Harriet first talked them into trusting her, reminding them that all their children were in the North now. Then she somehow found a wagon and a horse and hid them in the forest. She managed to put her mother's feather mattress on it. Then that night she walked her folks to the wagon and off they went. Again, miraculously, against all odds, Harriet delivered her parents to their freedom—by horse and wagon, both of them reclining on Mama's feather mattress.

For the next several years, Harriet personally escorted over one hundred slaves to freedom and helped liberate another two hundred slaves through a variety of ways. During the Civil War, she handled a raid that allowed eight hundred slaves to escape. She had many close calls, but she was never caught. She would say at the end of her life of her work as a "conductor" on the Underground Railroad, "I never lost a passenger."

Harriet settled in the town of Auburn in upstate New York. After the Civil War ended, she turned her talents to helping people in other ways. She began feeding poor people in her home, sometimes housing them as well. Any money she made she gave away, as she felt it was her Christian duty to do. She lived to be over ninety years old, and she died in Auburn.

Sometimes, in this world, the blessed person knows without a doubt why he or she is on this earth. Harriet Tubman knew that God had called her to deliver her people from a cruel fate at the hands of terribly misguided people. She knew God wanted her people free and that she was to be the instrument to get them to freedom.

Hundreds were saved from slavery and all its evils by Harriet Tubman, and they went on to live in freedom. Why? Because Harriet Tubman knew why she was here.

◉ Think…

1. Why do you think Harriet's father taught her so much about nature? Consider more than one reason.

2. Why did fellow slaves in Harriet's world decide to name her after her mother?

3. What Old Testament name did people secretly call Harriet Tubman?

◈ Imagine…

Think about where you live. Could you secretly steer people to the next town quietly, on foot, and in the dark? How would you do it? No GPS allowed!

◉ Get Creative!

Remember how Harriet sang to alert her family she was nearby and about to leave? Write a song that would tell your loved ones you are nearby. Make sure the lyrics include details only your loved ones would understand.

4

Mary Ann Shadd Cary

(1823–1893)

Self-reliance is the fine road to independence.

Mary Ann Shadd Cary

On an autumn day in Pennsylvania, a ten-year-old African-American girl looked up from her desk. She was a serious child with bright eyes and such a somber countenance that no one would ever know by looking at her how happy she was inside. Why so happy? Because, for the first time in her life, she was in school learning the most amazing things. Her parents had taught her to read and write, but now she needed more teaching, and she was getting it.

The child put down her pencil and looked out the window at the fall leaves. She thought about how in Maryland, where she used to live, it would be illegal for her to go to school because she was black. Here in Pennsylvania, however, it was not illegal, so she could get an education beyond what her parents could teach her.

"Is thee finished with thy work, Mary Ann?"

The child looked up, startled. The speaker was her teacher, a middle-aged white woman dressed in a brown dress with a white shawl across her shoulders and a white cap on her head. The blue eyes behind her spectacles were kind as she looked into the child's serious face.

"Yes, ma'am."

"Very well!" The woman's face broke into a bright smile. "Let us have thee read quietly while thy classmates finish."

The child's dark eyes lit up at the suggestion. She loved to read, and the Quaker teachers had such wonderful books. She rose quietly to fetch one.

The serious child was Mary Ann Shadd, born in Wilmore, Delaware. Her grandfather on her father's side was the son of a free black woman and a German soldier who had served under General Braddock in 1755 in the years leading up to the American Revolution. Her parents, Abraham and Harriet Shadd, were free and prominent black citizens of Delaware, and both were well-known antislavery activists. They used their freedom to help fellow African Americans in any way they could, though they needed to stay quiet about it. As a small child, Mary Ann often saw their home secretly opened to traveling fugitives on their way out of slavery.

Mary Ann was the oldest of what would eventually be thirteen Shadd children, and as the oldest sister, stepping up to responsibility would be second nature for her from the start. Determination and assuming leadership in order to make things happen were traits that would dominate the rest of her life. And she would be fearless about saying what was on her mind. Much like she might scold her younger siblings to keep them safe and well-behaved, the day would come when Mary Ann would scold her community, always with good intentions.

By the time Mary Ann was ten years old, her parents had become increasingly concerned because their children would not be allowed an education in Delaware. They knew that an education was too valuable to miss. So the family moved from Delaware to West Chester, Pennsylvania, so that the children could legally attend school. Pennsylvania was not a slave state, and the Shadd children would attend a school run by Quakers.

The Quakers were a religious group who believed in living a Christlike life to the best of their abilities. They also thought independently from many Americans in that they did not feel compelled to obey laws they felt were immoral or wrong. Since slavery was morally wrong, this meant Quakers did not believe in slavery and had no problem disobeying the laws of slavery. They answered to the laws of God over the laws of man, so it was God's laws they quietly obeyed. Consequently, the Quakers broke the law of the land to help hundreds of people leave slavery and move north to freedom.

The Quakers believed all human beings were equally worthy and that their freedom was God-given. The Quakers themselves treated everyone as equals. This was why, when the Quakers spoke, they addressed people with the formal words "thee" and "thou" instead of "you." Their intent was to show respect by treating everyone with extra dignity.

One of the many human rights the Quakers believed should be available to all was the chance to learn to read and write. They saw education as a means of improving a person and the world. There were public schools in Pennsylvania, but even there nobody was educating black children, so the Quakers stepped up to do it themselves.

The Quakers made a profound impression on young Mary Ann during her schooling. Once she adjusted to the unusual way they spoke, which sounded to Mary Ann like the Bible itself was speaking to her, she became an excellent student under their tutelage. She studied not only literature and writing and math but also philosophy and languages, all by age sixteen when she graduated. After Mary Ann graduated, she too became a teacher of her fellow African Americans.

While associating with Quakers in Pennsylvania, the Shadd family joined them in activities surrounding the Underground Railroad. This was an organized and secret group of many kinds of people, black and white, who worked quietly to help slaves escape from slavery and move on to freedom in the North. The Shadds let their home be a stop on that "railroad," and over the years Mary Ann became active in this movement as well. Some escaped slaves would stay in Pennsylvania, where the Shadds, the Quakers, and others would help them settle, or they would receive help in moving farther north.

But this activity changed on September 18, 1850. This was when Congress passed the Fugitive Slave Act. That was a shameful day for America. This new bill allowed Southern slaveholders to come to the North, hunt down any slaves who had escaped from them, and force them back to the South. Now there was no safe place in America for escaped slaves to build new lives and be free of the fear of capture. They could be kidnapped and taken away at any time. Even free blacks who had never been slaves were regularly kidnapped by men who lied and said they owned them. Clearly this made things unsafe even for the Shadd family.

The punishments for a slave's escape could be unspeakably harsh. Sometimes the slaves were taken back to the plantation and made to work harder than ever. Usually they were whipped. But sometimes they were maimed or even killed as a message to other slaves: *Don't try to escape.*

For many years Northerners had been able to ignore such cruelty going on in their own nation. But now they were presented with strangers on horseback showing up in their own towns, insisting formerly enslaved human beings in the community were personal property—and there was a new law of the land backing up those men and their kidnapping.

So escaping slaves no longer settled in Mary Ann's community in Pennsylvania. They still stopped there to rest on their journey and to receive aid, but then they moved straight on to Canada via the Underground Railroad. Canada had made slavery illegal in their country in 1833. Soon, this move across the border appeared to be the wisest thing for African Americans—and the Shadd family as well. Even though the Shadds were legally free, they would never be safe as African Americans—not as long as the Fugitive Slave Act legally allowed white people to kidnap black people.

At the time, in her early twenties, Mary Ann wrote an essay called "A Plea for Emigration or Notes on Canada West," in which she praised Canada for having already abolished slavery. She encouraged African Americans to move there in her essay, and in 1852 she followed her own recommendations. She moved to Windsor, Ontario, an area of Canada across the river from Detroit, Michigan, and taught school there.

Mary Ann was always one to lead the way, and indeed, her family followed her soon after. Many other African Americans did the same over the next ten years in order to be safe and live a normal life without fear of kidnappers. Between the passage of the Fugitive Slave Act in 1850 and 1860, the number of blacks in the sparsely populated provinces of Canada grew by twenty thousand people.

While in Canada, Mary Ann continued to lead the way and offer advice, even at her young age. She became a spokesperson to newly arrived African Americans. She founded and edited a Canadian newspaper called *The Provincial Freeman.* This weekly publication encouraged blacks to come to Canada from across the border to this place where they would be safe. Once they were no longer living in fear and uncertainty, they could concentrate on building an educated and independent life, something they couldn't have in the United States. Mary Ann lectured around Canada and the United States to gather funds for runaway slaves and to support her newspaper.

Mary Ann already had some powerful writing experience. Not only had she written "A Plea for Emigration or Notes on Canada West," she had also written a pamphlet one year before the Fugitive Slave Act containing an essay called "Hints to the Colored People of the North." In this, the young woman criticized many of the ways of her fellow black citizens. She said her goal was to "expose every weakness" of the black community that might keep them from overthrowing their oppressors themselves. What did she mean by that? While she knew black people were oppressed by the system of the day, she also felt they should not conduct themselves as victims. She felt they should look for any flaws in their own character and in their communities that they could fix.

At the time, not many people had access to reading this essay. Then Mary Ann wrote a letter to the famous abolitionist Frederick Douglass. In this letter, she criticized black clergymen. This was a bold thing to do, as ministers were usually the most important men in the black community. Douglass found this young writer's opinions engaging. A couple of years later, his newspaper *North Star* published excerpts from Mary Ann's "Hints" essay.

Since Mary Ann criticized some of the habits of her community in her essay, many readers became resentful in turn. Her intention was to get people to focus on education and moral refinement as they carved out their new lives in the North. She also strongly suggested those black communities become economically strong and not dependent on white economy. "Self-reliance is the fine road to independence," she said. And becoming independent was the best hope for the black community.

Mary Ann also wrote openly about organized black churches and the money spent on those churches and their ministers—money that could be used to better the community or educate individuals. She even criticized spending so much money on things like elaborate funeral processions. She challenged authority on a regular basis, and this caused much discussion among the *North Star* readers, most of it not positive toward Mary Ann. But Frederick Douglass himself was impressed. He would have a high regard for Mary Ann for the rest of his life.

She was, in a way, only a young American schoolteacher in a new country. But Mary Ann Shadd was so much more than that. Anyone who met her and looked into her bright and serious eyes could clearly see her high intelligence and passion. If they followed her actions, they could see her talents. She was taught by her family and by the Quakers to take the moral high ground, and that's what she did, without apology, in both her writing and

It is better to wear out
than to rust out.

—*Mary Ann Shadd Cary*

her speaking. Her intentions were good in that she wanted to see change in the institutions of faith and daily life for black people. Friends and family affectionately called her The Rebel. It was unfortunate for her, however, that often her abrupt style spoke louder than her well-chosen words.

And while Mary Ann spoke strongly in favor of racial equality, she also wrote about gender equality. This put her ahead of her time. She noted openly that women—black or white—were not treated fairly as human beings. Women could not be their full selves or in charge of their own lives. Even in the black community, women were expected not to express strong opinions. Mary Ann's world was not quite ready for these writings.

Eventually Mary Ann's unpopularity caused her to move her publishing operation to Toronto, Canada, where she was not as well known and could start over. Her brother and her sister lived there, and they helped her newspaper keep going.

In Toronto, Mary Ann met a man named Thomas F. Cary. He was an antislavery activist, a barber with his own business, and a widower with three children. Mary Ann was very impressed with Thomas and the feeling was mutual, and there is little else known about this relationship except that they married. Mary Ann was thirty-two years old, Thomas somewhat older.

Besides raising Thomas's children and continuing to write and speak, Mary Ann gave birth to a daughter, Sarah, and a son, Linton. But sadly Thomas and Mary Ann's time together was short. After only five years of marriage, Thomas died in 1860, just before his son Linton was born. Now Mary Ann was left with a newborn, a toddler, and Thomas's three teenagers to raise and support. The newspaper was no longer being printed, her husband was gone, and life changed drastically. It was a struggle, but Mary Ann had the resilience, the independent spirit, and the faith to handle it.

The next year, in 1861, the American Civil War broke out. Enforcement of the Fugitive Slave Act took a back burner as attention turned to the battlefields. From her home in Toronto, Mary Ann observed the progress of the war with great interest, since one of the main issues of the war was slavery. The Confederate Rebels of the South believed it was their right to have slaves; the Union Yankees of the North believed slaves must be freed and slavery must end throughout the country.

One day Mary Ann learned that the most astounding thing was happening: the Union Army was enlisting black soldiers to fight in the war. She decided it was time to go home and help. She packed up the children and moved the family to Washington, DC. There she worked at recruiting black soldiers.

In 1863 Abraham Lincoln signed the Emancipation Proclamation. This freed the slaves in Confederate states and made slavery illegal in every state. The war ended two years later. Mary Ann and her children stayed in Washington, DC, where she opened a new school for African-American children and continued to teach them.

When her youngest child, Linton, was nine years old, Mary Ann had a new personal goal: she wanted to become a lawyer. She knew she could impact policy and law if she were an attorney. So she became the first female student enrolled at Howard University Law School. She continued to teach school while she worked her way through law school—something highly unusual at the time. But she was not allowed to graduate. In order to become a lawyer, one must pass the bar exam, and Washington, DC, did not admit women to the bar. Momentarily disappointed but undaunted as usual, Mary Ann turned her talents to other things for the time being. She didn't give up. She simply waited, keeping her goal in mind.

Mary Ann Shadd Cary was one of the earliest voices to speak up about women and voting. This was called *suffrage*, which simply means the right to vote, and Mary Ann joined in the cause of women's suffrage. Under the Fourteenth Amendment to the Constitution, men could not be denied the right to vote based on race. But women, black or white, still could not vote. Being a woman in America meant depending on a man for income—husband or father—and even for safety. Women couldn't own property. In some cases, they didn't even have legal rights to their own children. Mary Ann developed legal arguments to expand the Fourteenth Amendment to include women. It would be many years before women got the vote, but Mary Ann was a strong part of the movement in its early days. She even worked with famous women's rights activist Susan B. Anthony.

Finally, at age sixty, Mary Ann was allowed to graduate from law school and take the bar exam. She became the first female African-American attorney in the United States, and she practiced law for several years in Washington, DC, focusing on women's rights. She became active in the effort to achieve women's equality in the workplace, and as a lawyer she fought against labor laws that were unfair to women.

She did many other impressive things during these later years as well. She founded the Colored Women's Progressive Franchise Association in DC in 1880, a club where African-American women gathered together in support for one another in any way necessary. She was also outspoken about the value of entrepreneurship—that is when private citizens take on or start their own business at some risk. Mary Ann always believed that this was how the black community would thrive and not be so dependent upon the white economy—an economy which so often was happy to take money from blacks but was not so willing to include them in the making of the money.

In spite of Mary Ann Shadd Cary's hard work for the equality of women, she would not live to see women given the right to vote through the Nineteenth Amendment to the Constitution. It was ratified in the twentieth century, but Mary Ann died many years before, in 1893, from cancer.

Her obituary described her as "a woman of excellent traits of character and loved by all who knew her." It went on to call her "eccentric at times," but concluded she was a woman "of kind disposition." It was a fitting description. Her daughter Sarah also praised her mother in an essay she had published. Apparently Mary Ann was as fine a parent as she was a worker for racial freedoms, gender equality, and other social concerns.

In Washington, DC, stands a simple brick house where Mary Ann Shadd Cary once lived. There is a plaque noting this on the building. It is located at 1421 W Street, and it is not open to the public.

But that seems somehow fitting. Mary Ann Shadd Cary was never looking for glory or attention. She was looking for progress. That brick house is a symbol—straight and strong, a reminder that a good woman stood equally straight and strong when, against all odds, she fought for the equality of not only her people but all people.

● Think...

1. What was the Fugitive Slave Act of 1850?

2. Where did Mary Ann suggest African Americans move?

3. What does *suffrage* mean? Whose suffrage did Mary Ann fight for?

Imagine...

Mary Ann was educated by Quakers who spoke in an old-fashioned way as a means of showing respect to one another. With a partner or two, research how to speak "Quaker." Then have a conversation with one another using the Quaker way of speaking. Does it help you better understand why Quakers spoke that way?

Get Creative!

What do you feel passionately about in the world around you? Do as Mary Ann Shadd Cary would do and write a journalistic piece about a change you'd like to see in your world.

5

Frances Ellen Watkins Harper

(1825–1911)

> **Jesus Christ has given us a platform of life and duty from which all oppression and selfishness is necessarily excluded.**
>
> **Frances Ellen Watkins Harper**

She was very small, but she was very smart. She had marveled at the books in her uncle's library ever since her parents had died and she had moved into her aunt and uncle's Baltimore home. Sometimes she would pull a heavy volume out, sit on the floor, and turn its pages. She could read some words but not a lot. She had watched Uncle William take a quill pen, dip it in a bottle of ink, and write beautiful letters. Sometimes he let her watch him teach in his classroom in a school he ran for other black children.

Every day she listened to her uncle and aunt talk with their friends, using words like *temperance* and *abolitionist* and other words she didn't understand.

But she wanted to understand them. They had made certain that she understood she was a free African American.

Other little girls played with dolls. But this little girl played with a pretend pen that she dunked in pretend ink so she could pretend to write.

Then Uncle William saw her playing like this and decided it was time. He said she was ready to be schooled. And she would start tomorrow!

A shiver of excitement ran down her spine. She could hardly wait!

Frances Ellen Watkins Harper was born to free black parents in Baltimore, Maryland, in 1825. Though her birthday of September 24 is known, for some reason the names of her parents are not known, even though they were free black citizens. They died when Frances was three, and she was taken in by an uncle and aunt, William and Henrietta Watkins, whose last name she took. They raised her as their own, and she spent a happy childhood with them.

The Watkins went on to have seven children of their own, so Frances was raised with a houseful of cousins. Her oldest cousin, a year younger than she, was William J. Watkins, who would become a famous abolitionist and would work with the great abolitionist Frederick Douglass. Her other cousins were named Richard, George, John, Henry, Henrietta, Robert, and Lloyd, all of them born between 1826 and 1845.

It must have been a stimulating household for the bright young Frances. Discussions in the Watkins household were most likely quite lively. Uncle William was a minister at the Sharp Street African Methodist Episcopal Church (AME), and he taught in his own school, Watkins Academy for Negro Youth. For over twenty years, Uncle William taught free black students a classical education. Her cousins Richard, George, and John would grow up to be teachers—and for a time, Frances would teach too.

Uncle William trained his students—and his children—on the issues of the day. Civil rights, slavery, and the controversial movement at the time for many black Americans to relocate to Liberia, Africa, could be topics of discussion in school and at the dinner table. The Watkins had friends who were Quakers, so there were also discussions about peace and what that meant in daily life and the world at large.

Frances was happy in this school, pleased to be one of a group of students ranging in number anywhere from fifty to seventy per year, male and female together. She learned the basics of education, of course. But she also learned to think logically and to express herself, particularly in writing. She studied with Uncle William until she was thirteen.

At fourteen, Frances found work in the home of a Quaker family. They paid close attention to this intelligent young lady and gave her free access to their amazing personal library. She was free to borrow any book. To a reader and a writer like Frances, this was a gift.

The Quaker family nurtured Frances's gift of writing. They encouraged her as she began writing poems. Soon Frances was sending her work to newspapers and getting published. Now she knew that writing was going to be her life's work. In 1845, she collected her poems and submitted them for publication. That collection became her first book of poems, titled *Forest Leaves*, or sometimes known as *Autumn Leaves*.

Five years later, when Frances was twenty-five years old, the Fugitive Slave Act was put into effect in the United States. This bill was a huge step backward for a nation calling itself free and united, because it allowed slaveholders in the South to come north to find enslaved people who had escaped from their plantations. Then the slaveholders were legally allowed to round up their escaped slaves and return them to the plantation. This was dangerous even for free blacks, especially in a slave state like Maryland.

The Watkins felt it best to leave Baltimore, where they were such a high-profile family. Frances agreed, though she did not go with them. She moved on her own to Ohio and taught sewing at a place called Union Seminary. She was safer in Ohio, but she did not stay there long. She simply needed more challenging work than teaching sewing. So in 1851 she moved again, this time to Pennsylvania to work with the Pennsylvania Abolition Society.

There she found great satisfaction in helping escaped slaves get to freedom along the Underground Railroad. She also got to know members of the Unitarian Church who, like the Quakers Frances knew, were active in the Underground Railroad.

Frances turned more attention to her writing at this point. It's what she liked best, and she became a successful professional writer—not the first African-American published writer, but certainly the first to make a living at it. In 1854, her *Poems on Miscellaneous Subjects* was published, and it sold very well.

Writing and working for the betterment of humanity was fulfilling for Frances. She was a single woman who in those days was called a "spinster." But she didn't mind. She had a full life and was able to pick up and move wherever she felt called. Then, when Frances was thirty-five, one could say love called—or rather, a widower named Fenton Harper called. They began a friendship that led to marriage in 1860. Fenton had three children, and Frances met her stepmothering duties with enthusiasm. In the third year of their marriage, Frances and Fenton had a baby girl. They named her Mary. It seemed like happiness might last forever.

But in 1864, after only four years of marriage, Fenton Harper died. Now Frances was the single parent to her toddler daughter and to her three Harper stepchildren. She grieved her husband but accepted her situation the best she could. After all, many women in America were losing their men in the war, so she was not alone. Right then it seemed like she lived in a land of widows. Frances gathered her children and kept them together.

When the Civil War ended in 1865, Frances found a new occupation. She aided blacks in the South in rebuilding their lives with their newfound freedom. This was during the Reconstruction of the South, where for the next ten or eleven years there was a window of openness and opportunity for blacks in America. Teachers and advisors, male and female, black and white, moved to the South to teach and instruct emancipated people in this time of huge changes and decisions on how to rebuild. Frances joined in with her abilities. African Americans were free, and in the South some blacks now owned land, went to school, and even ran for office. Frances toured the South and spoke to large audiences of both races. She encouraged education for freed slaves above all.

Eventually she made her way back to the North where she continued to write, often under the name Frances E. W. Harper. Besides her writing, Frances's professional life took off, especially for a black woman in the post–Civil War years. She was an activist and teacher.

Now that slavery was over, Frances became more involved helping women not only to get the vote but to lift themselves out of their unique kind of oppression. In her writing, Frances challenged women to be more spiritually minded than romantically minded. She challenged women to be less dependent on the affections of others. This was new thinking in these times. She worked these challenges into fictional stories. That way she could say what she wanted to say in the moral of the story.

In 1892, the book that Frances would be best known for was published—the novel *Iola Leroy*, which takes place during the Civil War and has a complicated plot of love and war and slaves and characters of mixed race. Her themes in that story have to do with what is known as "redemptive suffering," where one's suffering is for good. In this case, it was well known that slaves suffered. But Frances wanted the reader to know that Christlike suffering could enable a person to help redeem society of its ills. She wrote in a popular, very readable style, and readers enjoyed her books. But book critics treated her like a "hack" writer—someone who writes poorly and for money. *Iola Leroy* may or may not have been Frances's last novel, but it's the one that's remembered today.

As Frances grew older, she worked more locally for the downtrodden. In Philadelphia neighborhoods, she fed the poor and worked with troubled youth. She became involved in the Unitarian Church but also stayed involved in the AME Church where she taught Sunday school. She was raised in the AME Church, and she did not want to forget her upbringing or the history of her race—something the AME was more in touch with than the Unitarians. On the other hand, she appreciated the work for peace and reconciliation that the Unitarians were doing. She never did choose between the two, and today they both claim her as a member.

In 1909, Frances's daughter Mary Harper died. Two years later, in 1911, Frances died in Philadelphia at age eighty-six. Her funeral was in the Unitarian Church on Chestnut Street, and she was buried next to her daughter Mary in Eden Cemetery. They shared a tombstone, though over the years the tombstone was lost to view and eventually seemed to disappear.

After Frances died, philosopher and literary critic W. E. B. DuBois said of her writing, "She was not a great singer, but she had some sense of song; she was not a great writer, but she wrote much worth reading." Between that kind of left-handed praise and the dismissal of male critics in general, Frances would slowly fade from view in the American literary world for decades.

It seemed Frances Ellen Watkins Harper would be an unsung heroine. Her work was largely forgotten. But in the 1990s, *Iola Leroy* was reissued for a new readership. Her themes were once again explored and discussed. Today she is considered an early star in American literature and is called "the mother of African-American journalism." Her writings are no longer lost.

Her grave is no longer lost from view, either. When her new fans decided to give her a new marker, their digging in the dirt to erect it unearthed the original gravestone. What can be read from that gravestone is:

es Ellen W
Poet, Abolitionist
Her daughter
Mary

Partial birth and death dates are included. Most likely above her name would be the name "Harper," and one might wonder what word followed "Abolitionist." At any rate, her grave is no longer lost. Nor is her writing.

It's good that Frances E. W. Harper has been "found" again. She should be heard. Though she did not live to see women get the vote, she helped it come. She assisted untold numbers of people to freedom, from enslavement and oppression. She wrote eloquently about what was wrong and what was right in the land. And most of the money she made from her writing she poured back into helping those who needed it.

Frances Ellen Watkins Harper's first love—her writing—endures. Perhaps the last stanza of her poem "Bury Me in a Free Land" tells her readers what to remember of her:

> I ask no monument, proud and high,
> To arrest the gaze of passers-by;
> All my yearning spirit craves,
> Is bury me not in a land of slaves.

Think...

1. Who raised young Frances? Why?

2. What was Reconstruction? What did Frances do during the years of Reconstruction?

3. Which book of Frances E. W. Harper was reissued for a new readership in the 1990s?

Imagine...

Do you think Frances Ellen Watkins Harper and Mary Ann Shadd Cary met during their lifetimes? Think of a scenario where that could have happened. Where and why?

Get Creative!

Write a one-act play about these two women meeting. Remember, a play is mostly dialogue, so what do they talk about?

6

Anna Julia Cooper

(1858–1964)

> The cause of freedom is not the cause of a race or a sect, a party or a class—it is the cause of humankind, the very birthright of humanity.
>
> Anna Julia Cooper

The child dusted a china figurine carefully. She dare not break it or there would be trouble. This wasn't her own house; it was the master's house. Even though the child was small, she was expected to work, and this work was not difficult as long as she didn't drop anything. She could hear her mother outdoors beating rugs against a garden wall.

Suddenly she heard the gallop of horses coming toward the house, then voices and shouts, and the horses ran on by. Her mother ran into the grand house, then forced herself to walk. The child made eye contact with her mother, then watched her mother look around and start to weep.

"Baby," she said, "we're free."

Anna Julia Haywood was born into slavery on August 10, 1858, in Raleigh, North Carolina. Her mother, Hannah Stanley, was a slave who could read and write a little bit, more than most slaves. Anna lived her early childhood years with her mother, seven sisters, and two brothers on the plantation where she was born. It appeared that the plantation's owner, George Washington Haywood, was the father of the enslaved children, though it was never mentioned. The children were given his last name, but many slaves were given the last names of their owners. Regardless of her status in the master's extended slave family, Anna worked as a servant in the home at a very young age.

Anna was seven years old when the Civil War ended in 1865. After the war, there was a push in the nation to educate black children and adults in the South, teaching reading, writing, math, and even basic life skills that a system of enslavement had robbed from them. Schools of all kinds were made available to African-American students—from basic reading skills to classical education to trade schools to universities.

Anna received a scholarship to attend school at age seven. She was a student at St. Augustine's Normal and Collegiate Institution in Raleigh, a new school for blacks. The school was founded by the Episcopal Church Diocese with the mission to train teachers to educate former slaves and their families. They educated elementary through high school students plus offered some trade school classes.

Anna was very bright, and by age eight her superior intellect was showing. Today she would be called "gifted." At a very young age she was learning math and science, English literature, and the languages Latin, Greek, and French. She was such a fast learner that at age eleven she was given the task of being

One needs occasionally to stand
aside from the hum and rush of
human interests and passions
to hear the voice of God.

—Anna Julia Cooper

a "pupil teacher" at St. Augustine's—she helped teach the other students, most of them older than she was.

Like many schools at the time who accepted female students, St. Augustine's separated men and women into different classes, and they directed women down a different track of study than men. They even termed the track for females the "Ladies' Course."

But Anna didn't want to take these courses, which would be dumbed down for what the males in charge considered the "inferior" female mind. This also prevented females from pursuing higher education at a university. Anna fought for her right to take the same classes males took, and she did that by excelling, most likely to the point where she outshone the male students.

St. Augustine's also began training men for the ministry and preparing them to attend four-year universities. Anna met one of the scholars, George A. Christopher Cooper, who was from Nassau in the British West Indies and was a minister and professor of Greek. They fell in love and were married in 1877. As a wife, Anna was no longer allowed to teach.

Sadly, George died in 1879 after only two years together. Now Anna was a widow at age twenty-one. She began teaching again as a way to earn a living, though she would earn less than the male teachers. She also needed money to further her education. She entered Oberlin College in 1881 and once again had to fight to take the same classes as male students. She was successful in her fight and received her bachelor's degree. She returned to St. Augustine's to teach, then went back to Oberlin to earn her master's degree in mathematics.

By now it was 1887. Anna was not yet thirty, and yet much had happened in her life already. She'd been released from slavery, taught school, gotten married, become widowed, and now held a master's degree. What was next for this young woman?

Anna was invited to teach in Washington, DC, at the Preparatory High School for Colored Youth, soon renamed M Street High School. While there, Anna started doing what she would spend the rest of her life doing—presenting a positive image of African Americans to the world and sometimes to black people themselves. She joined a number of antislavery groups, abolitionist groups, women's rights groups, and self-improvement clubs. She worked to help students get access to the kind of education that would put them into higher education in better schools.

But she would soon notice something especially disturbing. It appeared that white schools who were allowing African Americans to enter and study didn't actually believe those students were capable enough for the track the white students were on. It was clear that these schools considered black people to have inferior intelligence and worked around that belief by offering a different level of education to their black students.

This obviously appalled Anna. But she also observed that even black educators saw women as having an inferior intelligence to men.

In 1892 she published her book *A Voice from the South: By an African-American Woman from the South*. She wrote, "I fear the majority of colored men do not yet think it worthwhile that women aspired to higher education ... the three R's, a little music and a good deal of dancing, a first-rate dressmaker and bottle of magnolia balm, are quite enough generally to render charming any women possessed of tact and the capacity for worshipping masculinity." Clearly Anna was not one to mince words.

For many years, Anna taught, wrote poetry and essays, and was a much sought-after speaker for groups with African-American concerns. She also spoke quite often for the Episcopal Church. She was known to be outspoken on the issue of an American educational system that simply did not consider the needs of black and female students. She spoke about this at the World's Congress of Representative Women held at the 1893 Chicago World's Fair. In a society very much run by white males, Anna knew she needed to stay on task at this point in her life to spotlight how to empower women, especially black women.

In 1915, one of Anna's brothers died, and she adopted his children. At a time when she was working her way through school and paying a mort-gage on a single woman's income, it was quite a commitment to take in five children—Regia, John, Andrew, Marion, and her namesake, Annie. They were young, too, with ages ranging from six months to twelve years. But Anna did this gladly and loved the children as her own. When her niece Annie died in her twenties from pneumonia, it was a tremendous loss for Anna.

In her sixties, Anna moved to France. She had contacts with French schol-ars who helped her get admitted to Sorbonne University in Paris. There she wrote two thesis papers, both in French, and in 1925, at age sixty-seven, she earned her PhD in history from Sorbonne. She was one of the first African-American women to earn a PhD. That may seem rather late in life to achieve such an accomplishment—yet Anna would live almost forty more years.

From 1930 through 1941, Anna was the president of Frelinghuysen Uni-versity in Washington, DC. She was tireless in her goal to give African Americans a solid education. She also made certain there were classes for employed African Americans who could not come to school during the day.

When the school faced eviction, she even held classes in her own DC home at 201 T Street. Today that Victorian house is on the African American Heritage Trail and is located beside what became Anna J. Cooper Circle.

In her later years, Anna became a prominent mover and shaker in the Washington, DC, African-American community. And although she was very old during the turbulent years of the Civil Rights movement in the 1950s and 1960s, she still was in the center of it. Imagine the authority she must have had in those years—she had actually been enslaved, and now she spoke on the civil rights of African Americans in a modern world. She never actually retired from speaking.

In 1964, Anna Julia Cooper died in Washington, DC. She was 105 years old. She asked to be remembered after her death as "somebody's teacher on vacation . . . resting for the Fall opening." Her funeral was held in a chapel at St. Augustine's College, and she was buried next to her husband in Raleigh.

In 1979, a stone was placed on her grave that reads in big, bold letters:

ANNA J. COOPER, PHD
1858–1964
EDUCATOR, AUTHOR, POET, AND
SCHOOL ADMINISTRATOR

EARLY ADVOCATE OF EQUAL RIGHTS
FOR BLACKS AND WOMEN

A GRADUATE OF ST. AUGUSTINE'S COLLEGE

Today not everyone knows who Anna Julia Cooper was. But any American who travels internationally has read her eloquent words. In the American passport, on the next to the last page, there is an engraving of the Statue of Liberty. On that page spread is a quotation from Anna Julia Cooper. It reads: "The cause of freedom is not the cause of a race or a sect, a party or a class—it is the cause of humankind, the very birthright of humanity."

Those are powerful words from a grand woman who was once a child slave. As a free and educated African American, she fought to secure her full rights and the rights of every American who had yet to be fully free. And she worked at that mission for—how is it possible?—almost a century. We can only hope to see someone like Anna Julia Cooper walk this earth again.

● Think…

1. What major events did Anna Julia Cooper live through in her very long life? Make a list.

2. How old (or rather, how young!) was Anna when she began teaching others?

3. Anna wrote her final two thesis papers in what language?

◆ Imagine…

Anna traveled to Paris to live temporarily and study. Is there a special place in the United States or in the world where you would like to live for a while? Where and why?

● Get Creative!

The passport office wants a quotation from you for the next passport edition! What can you write, in fewer than forty words, to inspire fellow Americans?

7

Mary McLeod Bethune

(1875–1955)

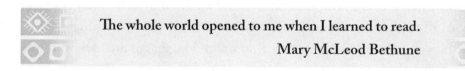

The whole world opened to me when I learned to read.

Mary McLeod Bethune

Patsy McLeod called for one of her daughters to help her with her laundry work. Patsy was the mother of seventeen children. On this day, in the late 1880s, she chose her ten-year-old daughter to come along and carry one handle of a large basket of laundry. The basket was heavy, but she knew her little girl was sturdy and strong. She worked in the fields like all the other children, alongside the adults, so she could certainly help carry the basket. They'd stop and rest along the way if necessary.

Mama Patsy took in white people's laundry for money. She boiled linens and clothes in huge tubs of hot water and homemade soap in the yard, hung the items on ropes to dry, and then ironed everything with a heavy iron she'd heated in a fire. It was hard, hot work. After she carefully folded the laundry, everything in the basket looked and smelled fresh and clean. Now the task was to deliver it. This Patsy and her daughter did on foot.

On this day, when they reached the customer's house they saw her two little girls playing in the yard with the most wonderful toys. The white lady told Patsy her daughter could go play with her own daughters. The child approached the white girls shyly, looking over their beautiful dolls and dollhouse and other toys, things she'd never seen before in all her young life.

Then she spied the books—big, colorful books with pictures and words that the child could not read. She reached for a book, but one of the white girls snapped at her, "You can't read that. Don't you touch that book with your black hands."

The child pulled back her hand, mortified. She returned to her mother's side and said nothing.

Years later she would remember that shaming moment and recall that it "did something to my heart." There were many ways black children were shamed at that time in the South. But the fact that she wasn't allowed to attend school and learn to read and write bothered this child more than anything else.

But she would not be bothered by that much longer. Against all odds, the very next year she would get her education. And everything changed.

Sam and Patsy McLeod were African Americans who had both been born into slavery but lived to see it end. During the years after the Civil War, the McLeods lived in Mayesville, South Carolina, where they worked on their own land and owned their small house, very unusual for Southern blacks at the time.

Their seventeen children were all born in the family cabin and given stirring and musical names as befitted the descendants of African royalty, which Patsy McLeod understood herself to be. The children were named Sally, Satira, Samuel, Julia, Kissie, Kelly, Carrie, Beauregard, Cecelia, Rebecca, Magdalena,

Hattie, Belle, William, Thomas, and Monday. And born in 1875—number fifteen in that lineup—was the family's favorite, Mary Jane.

Although Mary Jane McLeod was not born into slavery, some of her older brothers and sisters were and had since been freed with the other slaves in America. But free or not, the McLeod children were all born into poverty and illiteracy, the inability to read.

The McLeods were farmers who worked in the fields every day from sunrise to sunset—and if necessary, when the moon was full, they worked into the night too. Starting at age five, even Mary Jane picked corn and chopped cotton. They worked for area farmers for pay, but the good news was that the McLeods owned thirty-five acres of their own land, which they farmed mostly to feed the family. The large family continued to grow as Mary Jane grew, and her playmates were the children of her older brothers and sisters—her own nieces and nephews.

In addition to field and livestock work, mother Patsy McLeod took in white people's laundry. Mary Jane helped with this task too. It was tough living. But the McLeods embraced it anyway because of the independence they had. They loved their children deeply and taught them that prayer and hard work would get them by. And it did.

The McLeods were Christians who loved God. They owned a Bible they treasured and kept on a shelf for all to see. It was the only book they owned and an important book to have. But nobody in the house could read it. During slavery years, black people had been forbidden by law to read, and after slavery, there were usually no schools for them in the South. Clearly, reading was a powerful skill to have. It was a skill Mary Jane wanted.

It wasn't until Mary Jane was eleven years old that she finally learned to read. And as she would say years later, the whole world opened up to her once she could read. But how was it that young Mary Jane learned to read when so many other black children could not?

Most African Americans were not educated in those years after the Civil War. This was policy in the South and also in much of the North. So some church denominations built and taught in mission schools around the country in areas where people were too poor to build and support schools.

That's why, in 1886, a young black teacher from a place called Scotia Seminary moved to Mayesville in hopes of teaching black children. Word got out that teaching would be available, and the McLeods chose Mary Jane to go to school. They could not afford to have more than one child pulled from the fields, and the family members all agreed that there was something special about that sister Mary Jane.

So Mary Jane went to school. She walked four miles each way to get to the one-room schoolhouse, and the gifted young girl learned to read quickly. She was already known to be naturally bright in math—some white farmers had been using her to calculate accurately for them at the cotton gin. Now she could read too. Pretty soon she was helping the teacher with the younger children's lessons, and she was the first person in the McLeod house to read the family Bible.

She still worked hard at home. School was only in session a few months per year because local whites did not really want blacks educated, and they limited the amount of time black schools could be open. So between school sessions, Mary Jane continued to work in the fields.

One day the family's only mule died. It happened in the middle of planting, so it could have greatly affected getting the seeds in the ground, which down the line would greatly affect what the huge family would have to eat. But sturdy Mary Jane, age fourteen at the time, offered herself to "be" the mule for seeding. She hoisted the mule's harness over her own shoulders and pulled the plough through the soil to churn it up in rows as family members planted seeds behind her.

That same year, something wonderful happened. Thanks to her teacher, who could see such promise in her student, Mary Jane received a scholarship to attend boarding school in the next state. She would take her first train trip by herself at fourteen to travel to the Scotia Seminary for Negro Girls in North Carolina. This was so unlikely an opportunity for a black child in

Mayesville that it seemed to be a miracle. It was so miraculous that all the neighbors and friends of the McLeods showed up at the train depot at first light to see Mary Jane leave.

If Mary Jane was frightened the day she left home, nobody saw it. She knew this was a blessing. She stayed composed as she waited for the train to chug into the station. Neighbors joined her and the rest of the McLeod family on the train's platform. None of these people could read, and the idea that this bright child from their own community was going to get an education even beyond learning to read—well, it was a very emotional experience for all. She was not only the favorite of her family but was much loved by neighbors and members of the community too. Many of them—both family and friends—cried joyful tears as they put young Mary Jane on the train and said good-bye.

The train slowly moved out of the station, and Mary Jane watched her hometown for as long as she could. The rest of the eight-hour trip went by like a blur.

When Mary Jane arrived at Scotia Seminary that evening, she was confronted immediately with a strange, new world. She had grown up very poor, and she'd never been outside Mayesville in her life. So there were many new experiences for her that first night at Scotia.

It wasn't just that Mary Jane didn't know a soul. It was also that she had never been in a building higher than one story and never one built of brick. She had never climbed a flight of stairs. She'd never eaten at a properly set table. She'd never been around white people before, and now she was sitting at a table with them. She had never even used a fork before, so she asked the person next to her to please show her how. After dinner, she used her first toothbrush before sleeping in her first bed.

But she caught on quickly to those new things and new people. The bright and personable teenager became a favorite at Scotia just like she was at home.

The school had a philosophy—a stated belief—about how to teach African Americans who they knew would have to fight harder than white people to succeed. Scotia called it the "head-heart-hands" approach. It meant something like this:

Head: Study to build your intellect.

Heart: Grow your spiritual life with God.

Hands: Acquire practical survival skills so that you can maintain your independence.

This philosophy fit right into Mary Jane's very nature. This, after all, was the girl who had built her intellect by walking an eight-mile round-trip to get an education. This was the girl who had prayed and believed God would give her a way out of illiteracy and poverty and had shared the Bible's teachings with her family when she became able to read. This was the girl who, at fourteen, had pulled a plough through a field with the harness on her own shoulders so her family could eat. The "head-heart-hands" philosophy would be something she followed the rest of her life.

Mary Jane graduated from Scotia in 1893. By now, she had dropped the "Jane" in her name and went by Mary. She moved to Chicago to attend Dwight Moody's Institute for Home and Foreign Missions, eventually known as Moody Bible Institute, for the next two years. This was a school of Bible study and other studies in preparation for the mission field.

Mary felt she had been given opportunities so that she could offer them to others, and missions would be the way to do that. So after a missionary—a white man—who served in Africa spoke one evening, Mary felt led to go to Africa and teach. She let her teachers know this. Imagine her shock when she learned that her missionary board had a policy in which they would not send black missionaries overseas to teach black people, and that this was the policy of most missionary boards in most church denominations.

Why would they have such a policy? It showed how very deep prejudice about black Americans existed among white Americans, even among white Christian organizations. Did the board members really believe white missionaries would be better than black missionaries in Africa, based on race alone? Did the board perhaps think that black Africans would not accept instruction from other blacks—because the white board members themselves would not?

There was no explanation of the policy, but it held. Mary was deeply disappointed. She would one day say it was the deepest disappointment of her life.

But she moved on. She always felt she should not waste her time in negative situations but rather step around them and move on to better ones. Her life's philosophy could perhaps be summed up in one of the many spirituals she used to sing in the hot fields: "Nobody Knows the Trouble I've Seen." Mary liked to point out that really this was not a sad song because it ended in "Glory Hallelujah!" This kind of positive thinking was going to help this determined young lady move above her disappointment.

Mary moved back to the South and taught in her hometown for two years. She taught one of her brothers to read, which thrilled her just as much as it thrilled him. Now, when she was away, he could read the Bible to the family. It also meant she could write letters home.

Because Mary most certainly would leave again. If the door to teaching blacks in Africa closed, then she would teach black children in America. She shifted her thinking, and soon enough had a job teaching in Georgia. She stayed there for three years, developing her skills and her leadership qualities, and then she moved to Sumpter, South Carolina, for a new teaching position. While there, she met the man who would become her husband, Albertus Bethune. They met at choir practice.

Albertus was a teacher and sometimes a porter—and a good singer too. He and Mary fell in love and married in 1898. The following year they had their only child, a boy named Albert. Shortly after Albert's birth, Albertus took a job in Savannah, Georgia, and moved his family there.

Mary had lots of experience by now with good schools for black students, and she could see the Savannah school was lacking. She also had a dream—to

Faith is the first factor in a
life devoted to service. Without
it, nothing is possible. With
it, nothing is impossible.

—*Mary McLeod Bethune*

open her own school. She could offer black students so much more than they were getting. She could teach reading, science, math, and music. She could teach African Americans about their own heritage, something the Savannah school would not do. She wanted to teach young African Americans about how to deal with racism in daily life rather than sweeping it under the rug. She also wanted to promote work outside the school, knowing it was how black students—who did not have parents paying for their college—would survive and have economic independence. "If our people are to fight their way up out of bondage," she said, "we must arm them with the sword and the shield and the buckler of pride."

Albertus caught his wife's vision, and they left the inferior school in Georgia and moved to Florida, where they both took teaching positions at a mission school in Palatka. Now Mary could see the lay of the land and how they could offer a good school for black students in the area.

While in Florida, Mary observed that the part of the state where they were—northeastern, not far from the Atlantic Ocean—was growing in population because of the railroads. Workers were coming to Florida to lay track. At the same time, Floridians were beginning to see how tourism could be a boost for their economy, and trains were how tourists would get to Florida. This meant lots of workers and their families—including children—coming to the area.

Mary formulated a plan to start a school. It turned out, however, that Albertus did not really have an interest in start-ups. He preferred to teach and be paid a salary. He and Mary decided it would be best if he returned to Sumpter and taught there while she and son Albert stayed in Florida to build a new school. So Albertus moved back to his hometown. He did not return to Florida and passed away in 1919. Mary never loved another man after her husband.

With her son by her side, Mary got to work on building a new school for girls. She had grown up with nothing, so she was good at getting by with very little and at finding ways to use what others threw away. She found an abandoned shack on Daytona Beach, and Mary and little Albert lived in that shack as she made preparations to open her school. She hauled used lumber from a nearby dump to build things she needed. For money to live on, she baked sweet potato pies and took them to the railroad workers, who were usually Southern blacks and hungry for good down-home cooking. She would chat with the workers and get some idea as to what was happening and how many children were around her. She also sold life insurance. It appeared that Mary McLeod Bethune could do anything she put her mind to.

Indeed, in 1905, with very little cash, she opened her school in a rented, four-room seaside cottage. She started with five little girls and Albert, her big faith in God, and an impressive name: Daytona Normal and Industrial Institute for Negro Girls.

Did they have desks? Yes—made from cleaned up wooden boxes from the dump. Did they have writing utensils? Yes—pencils made out of pieces of charcoal and a kind of fountain pen made from charred firewood. For ink, they filled their "pens" with juice from dark berries that grew nearby. Mary was a very resourceful woman.

Mary used her "head-heart-hands" training right away. She liked to call this practical approach to true education "Greek and a toothbrush." The school even helped support itself by having the students grow and harvest their own food.

A master at getting positive attention for her school, Mary developed a choir with her girls and took them into expensive hotel lobbies to put on impromptu concerts, singing spirituals and folk songs. Then she would speak on-site about the school and ask for financial support. This went beyond taking up a collection. She even formed a board for her school made up of community people both black and white—unheard of in those times and in that area.

One day Mary had just spoken about needing funds to add a science building to her school when she was approached by an interested white man by the name of James Gamble. He was a millionaire, having started a company that sold items for cleaning and personal care that became known as Proctor & Gamble. James Gamble asked Mary more about what she needed. Then he decided to go see the school for himself.

Gamble's long black car pulled up to the beachside house where Mary was teaching. When Mary walked outside to greet Mr. Gamble, he looked around. "Mrs. Bethune," he said, "where is the school you speak of?"

Mary was ready for the question. "The school is in my mind, Mr. Gamble, in my spirit. I'm asking you to be trustee of a dream, trustee of the hope I have in my people."

Gamble looked around at the rolling waves, then back at the determined woman before him. He smiled. His good business sense, intuition about people, and personal sense of giving back told him to get involved—this woman was a winner. He not only became a trustee on the board and donated money but he also introduced Mary to other millionaires and philanthropists in the area.

She still had to struggle for funds at times, but the school grew to 250 girls, then high school grades were added, and then two years of college. Eventually the all-girls' school merged with the all-boys' school Cookman College. They stayed on Daytona Beach. Now it was called Bethune-Cookman College, and Mary McLeod Bethune was its president.

The college was known as superior, and eventually it became a four-year college. Dignitaries would come speak. And Mary turned her many talents to other things.

During this time, Mary wrote an impassioned letter to the Florida governor for the racist handling of the case of a black taxi driver murdered by two white men. The Florida governor paid no mind to her letter. But the First Lady of the United States did. Eleanor Roosevelt, wife of Franklin D. Roosevelt, heard about this brave black woman in Florida. She was impressed and wrote about her in her newspaper column.

Then Mary moved to Washington, DC, to accept a position in the New Deal offices. President Roosevelt was trying to handle the Great Depression, several frustrating years in which jobs were scarce and consequently so were food and necessities. In the process he developed many programs to put people to work and try to normalize the country. Mary took a government post as director of minority affairs.

She and First Lady Eleanor met in person and became good friends. Mrs. Roosevelt frequently took Mary's ideas to the president, and eventually the president spoke to Mary in person about issues. She had the ear of the president of the United States, and he listened to her. Washington, DC, turned out to be a great place for an energetic woman like Mary. She took on a number of causes and joined or formed new agencies for African Americans. She then became involved in the issues of American women in the military when America entered World War II.

She never slowed down until her health began to decline. Then it eventually became clear she could not be a long-distance college president, living in DC while leading the college in Florida. So she reluctantly shifted her position at Bethune-Cookman College to part-time and continued working for causes in the nation's capital.

Her son Albert married and had a child. This grandson was the joy of Mary's heart. And she was honored that the grandson—also named Albert—not only graduated from Bethune-Cookman College and then received his master's degree but also became a librarian—at Bethune-Cookman College! To think that the little girl who was chastised for touching a book now had a grandson who spent all his workdays with books.

Mary McLeod Bethune, educator and activist and grand lady, died in 1955 at the age of eighty. She left a legacy of education and activism that was so extensive it would be difficult to adequately trace. She was admired by so many that eulogies and columns praising her appeared all around the country.

It wasn't enough that Mary McLeod Bethune had an education. She wanted everyone in America, including and especially black people, to have an education too. She did her very best to make that happen—and along the way, she worked for the betterment of African Americans, and all Americans, in so many other ways.

It all started with a burning determination to read.

● Think…

1. How many children were born to Mary's family? What number was she in the lineup of children?

2. How did Mary help the family with the planting one year?

3. What did the "head-heart-hands" approach mean?

◉ Imagine…

Think of three books (besides the Bible) young Mary Jane would have been able to read once she had access to them. These would have to be available in the years she was living. Are they books you have read or would like to read?

◼ Get Creative!

When you think of a goal you have, how can you use your head, your heart, and your hands to make it happen? Show this in any way you wish—a chart, a picture, a poem.

8

Marian Anderson

(1897–1993)

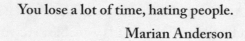

You lose a lot of time, hating people.

Marian Anderson

The choirmaster of the Union Baptist Church in South Philadelphia looked up from his musical score as the choir settled down. He needed another high voice for this piece, and the adult choir was short on sopranos right now. He looked around. His eyes landed on a young teenager looking back at him.

She had been invited to join the church's junior choir at age six. Even as a child, she had stood out. She was offered church solos and even outside invitations to sing. Now, the choirmaster patted himself on the back for pulling the girl out of the children's choir early and placing her in the adult choir at only age thirteen. Not only was she a strong contralto, the lowest female voice, with excellent pitch, but the girl could sing any part—soprano, alto, tenor, even bass if he needed it. He heaved a sigh of relief.

The young teenager watched the choirmaster with calm brown eyes in a serene heart-shaped face. He addressed her directly. "Sister," said the choirmaster, "would you kindly sing soprano for us today?"

"Yes, sir," she said. She had reached her adult height of five feet ten, and she stood with her back straight. She opened her music book and waited for the music to start.

This talented singer on the brink of becoming a young lady would be poised for the music to start throughout the rest of her life. Her phenomenal musical talent would cause her to become one of the greatest singers in the world, and her exceptional grace and dignity would allow her to open doors never before opened to African Americans.

Marian Anderson was born on February 27, 1897, and raised in Philadelphia, Pennsylvania, the daughter of John and Ann Anderson. John Anderson sold ice and coal for a living in downtown Philadelphia, and his wife was a former schoolteacher. The Andersons had three daughters—Marian was the oldest, followed by Alice and Ethel. All three girls were blessed with the gift of music, and all three would become professional singers. But it was Marian—who began singing when she was three years old and earned the nickname Baby Contralto—whose talent took her into an amazing singing career.

Marian's aunt Mary took charge of her niece's childhood singing, and this is mostly why Marian became a professional singer. She performed at other churches and local events even as a little girl, and Aunt Mary saw that the child was paid for her performances. To be paid a quarter or fifty cents to sing in the early days of the twentieth century was actually good pay and was a financial help at home. Later, in her teens, she could earn as much as four or five dollars for singing. At that time, grown men sometimes had to work two or three days to earn that kind of money.

Marian's father died in an accident at work when she was twelve years old, and after that her mother took in laundry to support the children. Life was hard, and the family was forced to move in with the Anderson grandparents. Marian became very close with her grandfather, a man who had been a slave. He died about a year after the family moved in.

This was a lot of loss for a girl in two years. So she leaned on her church and her choir for stability and comfort. As the oldest child in the family, Marian took her role seriously to be the one to keep things calm for her younger sisters. So she kept her emotions tucked inside for the sake of her family.

The family was unable to allow Marian to finish high school. It cost money to do that, and there simply was none extra. But the African-American church community stepped up to help. It wasn't only the choirmaster who saw Marian's extraordinary talent. Others saw it too. So the church community and choir started a collection called "Marian Anderson's Future Fund." They pulled together enough money for Marian to finish high school and to apply to music school. For the rest of her life, she would always remember that, talent or not, she got her start with the help of others.

But when she showed up to apply for admission to the Philadelphia Music Academy, the young admissions clerk looked at her and said, "We don't take colored." Then she bent back over her work.

Marian was shocked into silence. She had never been faced with prejudice in her young life. The African-American community in South Philadelphia was like a village, where people knew and took care of one another and treated people with courtesy. In the process, Marian had been shielded from racist interaction. Until now, she had even been treated as a favored child by her community.

She was stunned. She was especially surprised that the clerk speaking to her in such a disrespectful way wasn't much older than Marian. Didn't all young people think a little more progressively than their elders? Apparently not. Marian said nothing and left.

It was her way from her early years simply to move on from negative experiences, and that determination would bolster her throughout her life. If this school didn't want her, she would put her energy into finding a teacher who would take her—someone to help her develop her voice and her musical craft.

To her surprise, her church and its choir raised money again—this time for Marian to study with a respected voice teacher, Giuseppe Boghetti. When she auditioned for the teacher by singing "Deep River," he was so moved by her voice that he began to weep. What a joy it was for Marian to be trained by this fine teacher.

She worked very hard under Boghetti's tutelage. Her voice matured, her singing improved, and she learned to sing in several languages. She started winning singing contests and scholarships for more study. Eventually she was giving concerts around New York City, and in 1928 she performed at Carnegie Hall for the first time.

Eventually Marian felt she could get more musical education and opportunity in Europe. She moved to England and was well received by the British. She gave debut concerts (meaning the first concert in a particular city) in London, Berlin, and Salzburg as well as in the Soviet Union and the countries in Scandinavia and South America. Her concert in Salzburg, Austria, was particularly powerful. A famous conductor in the audience—Arturo Toscanini—approached Marian and said, "Yours is a voice heard but once in a century."

Touring around the world was so successful that Marian signed a contract for fifteen concerts back home in the United States. She opened the tour on December 30, 1935, at New York's Town Hall where she sang classical compositions but also African-American spirituals. Her deep contralto voice and powerful feelings behind it made singing spirituals a crowd-pleaser for the rest of her career. Critics in the *New York Times* now called Marian Anderson "one of the great singers of our time."

She gave concerts in states up and down the Atlantic seaboard. When she was in the South, however, it was dismaying to be the featured performer but not be allowed to walk in the front door of the venue or to stay in a hotel because of "Jim Crow" segregation laws—even when she was the third-highest concert box office draw. She began the habit of driving her own car whenever she could to avoid racial problems on trains or in waiting rooms. She also began staying with friends wherever she traveled to avoid being turned away by hotel staff.

The Jim Crow way of life was so strong in the South that when the Southern press wrote about her performances, the critics were not allowed to refer to her as "Miss Anderson." To give such a title as Mr., Mrs., or Miss to a black person was not done in those days in that area. It showed too much respect to a race of people the Southern white culture considered inferior. So the press referred to Marian as "Singer Anderson" or "Artist Anderson" or whatever other awkward term they could come up with so as not to say "Miss Anderson."

How did people outside concert halls in major world cities hear Marian in those early years? On the radio and in movie film shorts. These were the days before television or record albums or CDs, and families gathered together at home on a nightly basis to listen to the radio. They heard stories, news, and concerts . . . and they heard the great Marian Anderson. The singer of classical music became somewhat of a household name. Around the world audiences would see and hear her in movie theatre newsreels. The habit in those days was to show short films on current events, so audiences would on occasion see footage of Marian Anderson singing.

For the next few years after returning from Europe, Marian continued to tour the United States. During one tour, she and her German-American pianist Franz Rupp gave seventy concerts in five months. In these days of touring, Marian performed for US President Franklin Delano Roosevelt at the White House. She was the first African American to be invited to perform there—and then she was asked back to sing for King George VI when he visited the White House.

In 1939 Marian was invited by Howard University in Washington, DC, to perform in their concert series. Historically, Howard was a school mostly for black students, and it was exciting that Marian would be heard there. However, because of her national and international reputation, the organizers realized they'd need a larger venue than the school could provide. They knew the potential audience would be huge.

The organizers tried to rent a performance venue in DC called Constitution Hall, which would be large enough. It was owned by the Daughters of the American Revolution (DAR), a white organization. Blacks could attend events in Constitution Hall, though they always had to sit in a small section of the balcony. But when it came to performers, the DAR had a whites-only policy. Booking Marian Anderson was not going to happen.

First Lady Eleanor Roosevelt was a member of the DAR and was outraged by their refusal to allow Marian Anderson to sing at Constitution Hall because of her race. The First Lady actually resigned her membership and told the world about it in her newspaper column, "My Day." She said, "To remain as a member implies approval of that action, and I am therefore resigning."

The DAR didn't seem to care that the First Lady told the world about this overt racism. They did not budge on their policy.

Walter White of the National Association for the Advancement of Colored People (NAACP) suggested Marian sing outdoors instead. The First Lady got involved too, and the Lincoln Memorial, a national monument, was chosen as the outdoor venue. It also seemed appropriate because of the Civil War slavery issues when Lincoln was president.

On Easter Sunday, April 9, 1939, Marian Anderson took the arm of United States Secretary of the Interior Harold Ickes on one side and a military guardsman in formal uniform on the other. The two men led Marian down the monument's steps and onto a stage that had been built for the occasion. When Marian saw the crowd before her, she was glad she had a tight grip on these gentlemen lest her knees start to knock from nerves. There were an estimated seventy-five thousand people, black and white, waiting to hear Marian, all of them on their feet on the Lincoln Mall. There were no chairs.

Ickes introduced Anderson to the crowd. "In this great auditorium under the sky," he said, "all of us are free. Genius, like justice, is blind. Genius draws no color lines." Then he introduced the singer.

Marian was forty-two at the time, a lifelong performer, famous throughout North America, South America, Europe, and Russia. But she had never faced such a huge crowd. She later wrote about the moment in her memoirs. Her complicated feelings went well beyond stage fright. "I could not run away from the situation," she wrote. "If I had anything to offer, I would have to do so now. I had become, whether I liked it or not, a symbol, representing my people. I had to appear."

Marian's pianist began the opening for "My Country, 'Tis of Thee." Footage exists of this performance. In it Marian stands in front of the mighty statue of Lincoln, her heart-shaped face serene, masking the nerves in her stomach. She is dressed in a fur coat and a small fur cap on this chilly spring day. She looks out over the sea of hats, back and forth, and down at the front rows of radio broadcast microphones. Then she closes her eyes and begins to sing.

After her first song, she went on to sing five more songs, including "Ave Maria" and ending with the spiritual "Nobody Knows the Trouble I've Seen." Most of her performance that day was with her eyes closed, so that she would not see those thousands of people standing in front of her, or think about the millions more listening to her live performance on radio. She concentrated on delivering the music and interpreting it emotionally. It was a perfect performance.

At the end, she gave the audience her wide, beautiful smile flanked by deep dimples, and she waved. She had not planned to speak, but she did. She told the audience, "I am overwhelmed . . . I can't tell you what you have done for me today. I thank you from the bottom of my heart again and again."

Word of the outdoor concert and the circumstances behind it went around the world. Footage of Marian's performance was played in movie theatres everywhere. There was such an uproar against the DAR that they eventually apologized and changed their rules. Years later Marian would graciously accept an invitation from the DAR to perform at Constitution Hall.

In the summer of 1943, at age forty-six, Marian married a childhood friend, architect Orpheus H. Fisher. They managed to buy a farm in Danbury, Connecticut after a long search throughout the New York City metropolitan area of New York, New Jersey, and the rest of Connecticut. Even in the North, and even though Marian was a world-famous singer, white people did not want to sell their land to African Americans. Once the couple did manage to buy a small farm, they named it *Marianna*. They enjoyed the land and animals. Orpheus built Marian a studio in a separate building where she could rehearse. They did not have children together, but they were happily married for the next forty-three years and were privileged to grow old together.

Marian's singing career continued to flourish. During World War II, she entertained the troops overseas in hospitals and military bases. She always preferred singing concerts and recitals over singing live opera. She never felt she had the proper acting training to do justice to opera performed on the stage, but she did sing opera arias (pieces usually sung as solos) in several languages. She was excellent in those performances. Conductor Jean Sibelius told her, "The roof of my house is too low for your voice."

She especially loved singing African-American spirituals. Her contralto voice with its deep and beautiful range—often described as "velvety"—was perfect for that style of music, and she became especially known for singing those spirituals, for soaring and dipping her voice, then soaring again. But Marian said simply of such songs, "I love them because they are truly spiritual in quality; they give forth the aura of faith, simplicity, humility, and hope."

In spite of Marian's hesitation to perform opera on stage, in 1955 she debuted at New York Metropolitan Opera House (called the Met) playing the character Ulrica in Verdi's *Un Ballo in Maschera*. This was another first for Marian—she was the first African-American soloist featured at the Met, and she was met with a standing ovation the minute she walked onto the stage, before she sang a note. "I felt myself tightening into a knot," she later recalled. But of course, in spite of her nervousness, she sang beautifully and received another huge ovation.

This was the only time Marian would perform in a stage opera, and it was a powerful experience for her and for anyone who heard her. A *New York Times* reviewer wrote of the experience, "Men as well as women were dabbing at their eyes."

But just as satisfying to Marian was the fact that a mere twenty days later, baritone Robert McFerrin became the first male African-American Met soloist, singing in Verdi's *Aida*. These were huge steps for black classical musicians, and the entertainment world was blessed to finally get to hear them perform.

In the following years, the singer had many other accomplishments. In 1957, she sang at the presidential inauguration of Dwight D. Eisenhower, and she was named by President Eisenhower as a delegate to the United Nations. In 1961, she sang at the inauguration of President John F. Kennedy, and a few years later, President Lyndon B. Johnson awarded her the Presidential Medal of Freedom. She received honorary doctorate degrees from dozens of universities and was presented with a Grammy Award for Lifetime Achievement.

Marian decided to retire in her sixties. She started a farewell concert tour in 1964 that ended at Carnegie Hall in April 1965. After that, she enjoyed a quiet life with her husband on their Connecticut farm. She was often seen around town in Danbury, and she stood in lines and waited for service just like anyone else. She never wished to attract attention. Known as quiet and humble, Marian was always a far cry from a musical diva.

She wrote her memoirs in a book called *My Lord, What a Morning*. She made many musical recordings. She also made a recording telling the story of her black cat, Snoopycat. The cat was a barn cat at the farm, and she brought him indoors for a pet. Her rich, warm voice sang Snoopycat's story with light, charming songs, and between the songs she told all about their adventures together.

Marian and her husband, Orpheus, had a good long marriage until he died in 1986. Marian then sold half the farm's acreage and continued to live on the remaining fifty acres, leaving from time to time to attend special events and sometimes to accept awards. Eventually, as her health failed with age, she moved across the country to Portland, Oregon, to live with her nephew James DePriest, who was a well-known concert conductor. On April 8, 1993, she died at his house. She was ninety-six years old.

Marian Anderson's memorial service was held at Carnegie Hall in New York City. Over two thousand people attended. The focus of the service was on Marian's singing rather than on her as a person. Attendees in particular appreciated hearing recordings of those spirituals that best expressed Marian's faith in the dark times and the bright times, songs she was known to love to sing, from "Sometimes I Feel Like a Motherless Child" to "He's Got the Whole World in His Hands." She was buried in the family plot alongside her loved ones.

The world was given a gift with the rich, expressive voice of Marian Anderson. But the world was also gifted with a role model. She wrote, "The knowledge of the feelings other people have expended on me has kept me going when times were hard. . . . The faith and confidence of others in me have been like shining, guiding stars."

Her nephew James DePriest credited her success not only to her talent but also to her ever-present faith and dignity. She simply would never give in to hate. "You lose a lot of time, hating people," she was known to say. She believed it was her duty to move forward in love, not only because Christ teaches us to love but also because love opens doors.

Among the many things she accomplished in her amazing life, Marian Anderson often contributed her service to the Civil Rights movement in her later years. But if asked, she would not have called herself an activist. Instead, she believed that if she performed and behaved with dignity, prejudice might go away.

Prejudice did not go away. But without a doubt, the faith and dignity of Marian Anderson broke down barriers for all artists and performers of color.

Think...

1. What was "Marian Anderson's Future Fund"?

2. What was "Jim Crow"?

3. Why did Marian Anderson drive her own car to concerts?

Imagine...

Besides her serious undertakings, Marian also surprised her fans by singing about her cat, Snoopycat. Do you have a surprise talent or interest that you would like to share with your world? Write about it in your journal or talk about it in a small group.

Get Creative!

Watch an online recording of Marian Anderson singing in front of the Lincoln Memorial. Pretend the statue behind her is alive for a moment—what is Mr. Lincoln thinking? Write an internal monologue for him as he views what's going on.

9

Mahalia Jackson

(1911–1972)

 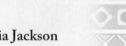 Faith and prayers are the vitamins of the soul. Man cannot live in health without them.

Mahalia Jackson

On a late October day in New Orleans, Louisiana, a baby girl came into the world. She was the daughter of Johnny and Charity Jackson. The baby's father left her mother shortly after the child's birth, so Charity and her baby girl moved into a house full of her relatives living on Pitt Street in a section of New Orleans known as Black Pearl.

At birth, the baby had a condition people called "bowed legs" and doctors called *genu varum*. While she was still an infant, doctors wanted to break her legs and put them in casts to straighten them as they grew.

The house Charity moved her baby to was full of extended family, most of whom were women with opinions. The surgery option was discussed by all and then rejected. Maybe it just felt wrong to imagine a doctor breaking a baby's legs. Or maybe, in the New Orleans of 1911, African Americans had a strong distrust of white doctors.

Whatever the reason, there was no surgery. Instead one aunt suggested a natural technique. Charity should rub the baby's legs with used dishwater, the greasier the better. She did that for a long time. This did nothing at all, and the child would have bowed legs all her life.

Fortunately, the condition of her legs never slowed this child down. Since women did not wear trousers in those days, and skirt hemlines were fairly long, as the girl grew up her condition often did not show. And it certainly never kept her from doing anything. She could play outdoor games with other children. She could do her chores around the house. She could even dance, sometimes entertaining white ladies her mother cleaned house for.

But the best thing about this child had nothing to do with her legs. She loved to sing, and she could sing gloriously. One of her aunts predicted the girl would grow up to be famous and would sing before kings and queens.

And one day, she did.

She was born Mahala Jackson (she would add an "i" to her name later on), and from the beginning she was called Halie. She was named after her mother's Aunt Mahala, whom the family called Aunt Duke. This was a nod to the fact that she was the matriarch of the family—the woman with all the power—and extended family members lived with her in her three-room house.

New Orleans was known for its small houses lined up next to each other on residential streets—houses called "shotgun." They had a total of three rooms that led into each other without hallways from front door to back door—a living area, a bedroom, and a kitchen. People called it "shotgun" because one could shoot a gun straight through the house without hitting a wall.

When mother Charity and daughter Halie moved to the family shotgun house, there would now be thirteen people and a dog living in those three rooms. It was lively and crowded, and these were not quiet people. The relatives living there at any given time were Halie's brother Peter, Aunt Duke, Aunt Isabell, Uncle Boston, Uncle Porterfield, Aunt Hannah, Aunt Alice, Aunt Bessie, their children, and Halie's respected grandfather, Reverend Paul Clark, a former slave.

Since Halie's father, John Jackson, remarried shortly after he left her mother, Halie gained several half siblings from that marriage. She was not raised by her father but she most likely was gifted with talent from his side of the family. Her Aunt Jeanette and Uncle Josie were vaudeville players. Vaudeville was a kind of entertainment that was popular in America at the time. In downtown theatres or countryside tents, performers sang, danced, and acted in funny skits. It was a cheery entertainment for people during hard times.

In the home, radio was the big entertainment. The most popular blues and jazz singer on the radio then was Bessie Smith, nicknamed the Empress of Blues. Halie heard the popular singer often on the radio in the shotgun house. She learned some of her singing style by listening to Bessie Smith, and she would be compared to her vocally later on.

Sadly, when Halie was only five, her mother died. Aunt Duke took responsibility for Halie and Peter. But now that their mother was gone and the powerful Aunt Duke was in charge, for some reason they were mistreated by her. She forced the children to work as much as she could, and she would beat them if she wasn't satisfied with their work. If other relatives didn't do their chores—and with that many people in such a small space, there were many chores—Halie and Peter were expected to pick up the slack. Halie loved school, but Aunt Duke wanted her to work instead of go to school. So Halie dropped out in the fourth grade. She was always dismayed by this turn of events.

But singing kept her soul going, and Bessie Smith aside, Halie preferred to sing gospel songs and to sing them in church. Halie's natural ease with an audience could partly have been inherited from her father's vaudeville relatives, but her true training came by singing from a very young age in the local Mount Moriah Baptist Church on Wednesdays, Fridays, and four times on Sundays. Halie was a believer in Christ from an early age, thanks to Mount Moriah, and she was baptized by her pastor in the Mississippi River.

Halie continued to try to keep out of Aunt Duke's disfavor as she grew up, and she continued to sing in church. She developed a powerful contralto voice (the lowest range for women), and she could be heard outside during services all the way down the block. She sang in an enthusiastic style with hand-clapping and abandon.

As she grew to become a teenager, some people expected she'd move into singing jazz or blues—it was New Orleans, after all, the birthplace of this American style of music, and many blues musicians developed their style from growing up in church.

But New Orleans was also the home of gospel music, and that's what Halie sang and would always sing, without exception. God fed her soul. She would say, "I sing God's music because it makes me feel free. It gives me hope. With the blues, when you finish, you still have the blues."

Starting around 1916, the United States began to experience what historians now call the Great Migration. This was when African Americans left the South and moved north to cities such as Detroit, Chicago, Philadelphia, Cleveland, and other cities with factories. Up north, a factory wage could be three times more than a black person could earn by working the fields in the hot sun down south. It also meant starting over in an area of the country not as affected by the history of slavery, so there would be more employment and housing opportunities for blacks.

This migration went on for many years, through World War II and beyond. In the end, around six million African Americans started over in northern cities. With that move came new neighborhoods where blacks maintained a kind of village life together. And with that social world came new entertainment. Jazz and blues had also moved north.

When Halie turned sixteen, in 1927, she joined that Great Migration and left her beloved New Orleans. At the time, Aunt Hannah was living in Chicago. She came to New Orleans for a visit and quietly pulled Halie aside. "Do you want to come home with me?"

What an opportunity! It was a tough decision for one so young, but Halie was old enough to know that without an education, in the South, her future as a black woman would be one of cleaning white people's houses and taking care of their children. She wanted more than that in her life. Plus Chicago sounded exciting!

Halie said yes.

"Okay," said Aunt Hannah. "But don't tell your Aunt Duke I asked."

The day Halie left home with Aunt Hannah, all the relatives said good-bye on the front porch on Pitt Street, and all were crying. Even hard Aunt Duke cried. But Halie knew this was the right move, and she boarded the train for Chicago with Aunt Hannah and with high hopes.

In Chicago, Halie immediately looked for work. She had a golden voice and could have made a good living even at sixteen by singing in bars and clubs. Labor laws then were much looser for a working teenager. But she would not do it. Halie believed strongly that her voice should only be singing God's music. She would sing in churches and concert halls over the years, but never in bars and clubs—and never music that wasn't God's music. This was a stand she took early on and never stepped away from for the rest of her life.

Halie quickly found a church to attend—Greater Salem Baptist Church. On her first Sunday, somehow she managed to sing a solo—one of her favorite songs, called "Hand Me Down My Silver Trumpet, Gabriel." It was so well received that she was asked to join the choir and tour the area with them. She also soon joined and toured with the Johnson Gospel Singers, a professional group. She loved singing with the group, and she was paid for it too. So she could make a living on that while staying with Aunt Hannah.

Within a couple years of singing gospel in the Chicago area, Halie met the great gospel music composer Thomas A. Dorsey. They developed a music relationship in which he gave her advice and suggested songs for her to sing. They eventually toured together for many years. Dorsey composed the song "Precious Lord, Take My Hand" for her to sing. That song would become the most requested song of Halie's throughout her career—what was called her "signature" song.

By her early twenties Halie was such a well-known gospel singer in Chicago that she signed recording contracts and made records. She was developing a strong and beautiful voice as she sang professionally and picked up advice and technique wherever she could. But she also showed herself to be a strong and generous young woman, kind, personable, and fun. She addressed her many friends as "baby." In 1931, she added an "i" to her name and now became known as Mahalia Jackson, although over the years she was known to introduce herself as, "Just Mahalia, baby." It was her way of saying, "I'm no more important than you. We're all the same in God's eyes."

One of Chicago's popular radio disc jockeys was a white, Jewish journalist named Studs Terkel. He was involved in a lot of Chicago life, and he had a radio show where he played music of all kinds—American folk, blues, some classical. His listeners were mostly white. In the early part of the twentieth century, racism existed even in what was played on the radio. Studs would play whatever he liked no matter what race or nationality the musician was, but he was unusual that way.

One day in the 1940s, in a record store, Studs Terkel heard a recording of Mahalia Jackson singing "Move On Up a Little Higher." This was another of Mahalia's favorite songs. Black people in Chicago knew the song, but white people did not. Studs had never heard it before, and he had never heard such a voice. He bought the record and played it the next night on his radio show. He was the first white disc jockey to play Mahalia on the radio, and really even the first to play black gospel to a white audience. Almost overnight Mahalia had a white audience added to her black audience.

Then Studs went to the Greater Salem Baptist Church to meet Mahalia and hear her sing live, and he was blown away. He continued to play Mahalia's song on his show, and her record sales shot up. Stores couldn't keep the record in stock, and it sold an amazing eight million copies.

Best of all, Studs and Mahalia became lifelong friends. "Studs," Mahalia would say, "you're the one who led me to the white world." But Studs disagreed; he felt she was so good that whites would have found her anyway. He would say, "I'm a Jew, but if anyone could lead me to Jesus, it would be Mahalia."

Now Halie from New Orleans was the great Mahalia Jackson, known worldwide as "The Queen of Gospel." The city of Paris, France, called her "The Angel of Peace." Her recording of "Silent Night" as a single became Norway's bestselling record ever. She would eventually record thirty albums. She was the first black gospel artist to sing at Carnegie Hall in New York City. It was as her aunt predicted all those many years ago—Mahalia indeed sang all over the world, even for royalty. Singer Harry Belafonte claimed she was "the most powerful black woman in the United States." She made good money as a singer and gave a lot of it away or invested it in Chicago real estate and businesses.

Civil rights issues were stirring in America in the fifties and sixties. Mahalia got involved financially, personally, and musically. Her life as a black woman was indeed better in the North than if she'd stayed in New Orleans.

But even in Chicago she found something she would call "peculiar." It was the divide between her life as a famous entertainer and her life as a regular black citizen. When she was on the stage and backstage, white people would be so warm and smiling toward her. They would even hug her. But on the street or in stores, where people didn't recognize her, she was treated by whites like any other African American. That treatment was often rude and dismissive. She was ignored by white staff in stores or restaurants. She had trouble hailing a cab as a black woman. But when she performed as "Just Mahalia," white people adored her and treated her with the utmost respect. It was unsettling.

She saw blatant prejudice when she shopped for a house in Chicago. She was constantly turned away in white neighborhoods, even though white Realtors and white homeowners knew she was an internationally famous singer of

God's music. When she finally purchased a house in a white neighborhood, her windows were shot out. Then, one by one, all the white homeowners in the neighborhood moved away. Mahalia stayed. Black families bought the houses left behind.

Fortunately Mahalia had her feet on the ground and her faith intact. Obviously she didn't like what she experienced regarding race, but she kept on living with dignity. Then she found an outlet for that frustration as a civil rights activist. She met Dr. Martin Luther King Jr. and his associate Ralph Abernathy. She sang at events when Dr. King spoke, and she sang his very favorite song whenever he requested it, "Precious Lord, Take My Hand."

She joined King and Abernathy at a rally in Montgomery, Alabama, where she sang "Move On Up a Little Higher" and a couple more songs. It was a successful rally and raised money for the movement. But while they were at the rally, Abernathy's home was bombed. Mahalia continued working with the movement regardless.

In 1963, she joined the March on Washington for Jobs and Freedom— known by its shorter title as the March on Washington. This was one of the largest rallies for civil rights in American history. Estimates of between 200,000 and 300,000 people, black and white, gathered in front of the Lincoln Memorial. Mahalia Jackson performed two songs: "How I Got Over" and "I Been 'Buked and I Been Scorned."

There were many speakers at this event, including Dr. Martin Luther King Jr. He gave a stirring speech in which he talked about the Constitution and how America had failed her people. Like many speakers and preachers, he had given this speech before, and since Mahalia often traveled with him, she knew his speeches. As Dr. King neared the end of his speech, Mahalia Jackson shouted from the crowd with her powerful voice, "Tell them about the dream, Martin!"

Dr. King heard Mahalia loud and clear. He immediately abandoned the rest of his prepared speech and spoke his soon-to-be-famous line, "I have a dream . . ."

During her activist days, Mahalia was able to pay a little back to journalist and friend Studs Terkel for his part in her success. She called him up one day and said, "Come on over. Martin wants to talk to you." So Studs went to Mahalia's house, found the great civil rights leader in his stocking feet and exhausted, and learned that actually Dr. King had never heard of Studs.

But since Studs was Mahalia's friend, Dr. King graciously granted an interview regardless of his fatigue. Studs knew he never could have interviewed this great man had Mahalia not fixed him up. He never forgot it.

While rallies and activities to promote civil rights continued, the more visible leaders' lives were often threatened, and the same was true for Mahalia. But she continued showing up and donating money and singing. She said she always hoped her music "could break down some of the hate and fear that divide the white and black people in this country."

Then came the huge blow to the world and certainly to Mahalia when Dr. King was assassinated in Memphis in 1968. Mahalia sang his favorite song at his funeral, "Precious Lord, Take My Hand."

Mahalia's reputation continued to grow and her career took new turns. She recorded with orchestras, sang in concert halls and folk festivals, and performed at President John F. Kennedy's Inaugural Ball. She had singing parts in Hollywood movies. She established scholarships, opened small businesses, and won awards. It was a fast-paced, satisfying life for her.

But in January of 1972, at age sixty, Mahalia Jackson died in Chicago. She had some chronic health problems that led to heart failure. The entire world mourned her passing with tributes.

Both Chicago and New Orleans memorialized Mahalia. In Chicago, her body lay in a mahogany, glass-topped coffin in the Greater Salem Baptist Church, where estimates say 50,000 people filed by her in quiet tribute. The next day there was a two-hour funeral service with many notables present, including Coretta Scott King, who spoke, and singer Aretha Franklin, who sang "Precious Lord, Take My Hand."

A few days later there were more memorials in New Orleans, with long lines of mourners filing by her coffin. Then the funeral procession, which boasted twenty-four limousines, drove by Mount Moriah Baptist Church where little Halie Jackson had first started singing in public with that big, beautiful voice. Finally the procession drove to the cemetery where, in New Orleans fashion, Mahalia's coffin was put in a small tomb aboveground.

Mahalia had been generous to both people and causes while she was alive. Now her generosity extended to the distribution of her substantial wealth after death. Mahalia had no children, and most of her estate went to her beloved relatives who had helped her along the way—in particular, her Aunt Hannah who helped her move to find the full life Mahalia wanted to live.

Mahalia Jackson's powerful and unique voice changed the world of gospel music. Today both black people and white people listen to and sing black gospel songs, and it started with Mahalia's recordings. She opened up for the world a style of singing that glorified God. And as a woman, she backed up what she sang by living a good life—one that was directed by Christ.

Mahalia Jackson lived her favorite song—she did indeed "Move On Up a Little Higher" every day until she left this world. She soared above the poverty and abuse of her childhood. She cared about others enough to put her life in danger to fight for their well-being.

In the end, Mahalia Jackson was far more than "Just Mahalia."

◉ Think...

1. When Mahalia Jackson moved to Chicago, she had a favorite song she sang in church. What was it?

2. What was the Great Migration? What cities did it affect?

3. Which song did Dr. King especially like Mahalia to sing?

◆ Imagine…

There are a few occasions during the Civil Rights movement where singers Mahalia Jackson and Marian Anderson most likely met. When were those times? Pretend you were at their first introductions to each other. What do you think they said to one another?

■ Get Creative!

Find a recording online of Mahalia Jackson singing the song "Move On Up a Little Higher." Pretend you have your own cable television show (what's your TV name?) and you want to tell people about this singer you've heard for the first time. How do you describe her to the audience? Remember, you're on TV!

10

Rosa Parks

(1913–2005)

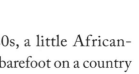

> I would like to be remembered as a person who wanted
> to be free . . . so other people would also be free.
>
> **Rosa Parks**

Outside of Montgomery, Alabama, in the early 1920s, a little African-American girl and her younger brother walked to school barefoot on a country road. They had been homeschooled by their mother until she felt it was time for them to go to a public school. And although the girl had been eager to attend school, it had turned out to be a disappointing experience.

School was a short season for black children, for one thing. Black families had to work hard and pull together to survive, so black children only attended school when they were not absolutely needed to work in the fields. School attendance was not a priority for most black families. The local government that offered education for children did not include funding for black children. The black community, already financially stretched, was on its own.

So the little girl discovered that school for black children was very grim. The one-room schoolhouse was old and shabby and had no desks inside, only benches. There were windows but no glass in them. If the weather was cold, the children had to bring wood from home to keep a wood-burning stove going. There were never enough books, and those they had were almost worn-out from use.

White children attended school in big brick buildings full of windows and light. Each child had the books he or she needed. And school buses transported white children to school for the nine-month school year.

Every day that the little girl and her brother attended school, they would walk the miles there and back in any weather. Keeping alongside the road, they would see shiny school buses roar by. Usually the white kids on board paid no attention to the two black children on the side of the road. But sometimes the white kids would open the bus windows to laugh at them or even to throw garbage at them.

This was demoralizing. Inside the little African-American girl, a righteous anger started to grow. And so did a strong sense of justice.

One day, she hoped, things were going to be different.

In February 1913 in Tuskegee, Alabama, in a wood-frame house with a front porch, Rosa Louise McCauley was born. She was the firstborn child of James and Leona McCauley. James was a carpenter who traveled with his brother building houses all over the South. Leona was a schoolteacher who wanted a stable home for her family. Unfortunately James preferred being on the road rather than at home, and shortly after their second child, Sylvester, was born, the parents decided to separate. Rosa saw her father one more time when she was five and not again until she was an adult.

Leona took her small children and moved in with her own parents near the small town of Pine Level, not far from Montgomery, Alabama. That's where Rosa and her brother grew up on the small farm their grandparents owned. Life in the country was great fun for children. They enjoyed playing with the farm animals and climbing trees in an orchard full of fruit, pecans, and walnuts. They helped milk cows, fetch eggs, and fish the river for the supper table.

The family members all belonged to Pine Level's African Methodist Episcopal (AME) Church, a congregation that could only afford to share a minister. That minister preached in Pine Level on the third Sunday of each month. The other Sundays, the family went to church anyway by attending a local Baptist church. Every evening at home, the Bible would be read aloud, and Grandpa would lead them all in prayer.

Rosa learned early on that the Bible was important. Grandma's eyes were too bad for reading, so from an early age Rosa, who had been homeschooled by her mother, read the Bible to her grandmother. In the process, the child chose and memorized her favorite Scripture passage, Psalm 27:1–7.

> The Lord is my light and my salvation; whom shall I fear? The
> Lord is the strength of my life; of whom shall I be afraid?
> When the wicked, even mine enemies and my foes, came upon me
> to eat up my flesh, they stumbled and fell.
> Though an host should encamp against me, my heart shall not fear;
> though war should rise against me, in this will I be confident.
> One thing I have desired of the Lord, that will I seek after; that I
> may dwell in the house of the Lord all the days of my life, to
> behold the beauty of the Lord, and to enquire in his temple.
> For in the time of trouble he shall hide me in his pavilion; in the se-
> cret of his tabernacle shall he hide me; he shall set me up upon
> a rock.
> And now shall mine head be lifted up above mine enemies round
> about me: therefore will I offer in his tabernacle sacrifices of
> joy; I will sing, yea, I will sing praises unto the Lord.

> Hear, O Lord, when I cry with my voice: have mercy also upon me,
> and answer me.

Rosa would return to this passage often in the difficult years to come.

Grandpa and Grandma taught Rosa and Sylvester about their own roots and about when they had been enslaved and when they were freed. They also made sure the children knew who their four great-grandparents were from that side of the family. One great-grandparent was a slave directly from Africa, one was a white plantation owner, one was an indentured servant from Ireland or Scotland, and one was half African, half Native American, so there was quite a bit of white blood in their background.

Nevertheless, the grandparents instructed the children not to trust white people and to avoid them at all costs. Grandpa and Grandma did not even want the children to play with white children, something that was usually acceptable until a certain age. The old folks had seen too many childish games turn into fights and subsequent racial issues. Best not to mix.

This was all a little puzzling to Rosa since her grandparents were not only kind, peaceful, Christian people but also expressed no fear of anyone, white or black. All her life she would remember being at her grandparents' house when they learned that the Ku Klux Klan was on the hunt for someone. Word always got around among the black community when something ugly was expected to happen. Rosa recalled her grandfather sitting at the door all night, his rifle at his side, as Klansmen on horseback galloped furiously right past the house. She never sensed fear from Grandpa. But he was ready to protect his family if he needed to. That was his bottom line.

So between the pride and fearlessness of her family and her faith in God, Rosa grew up with a strong sense of who she was and who she was not. She obeyed the family request that she avoid white people. That would not always be the case, but it was during the first half of her life.

Rosa had bad health during her younger childhood years, but an operation to remove her tonsils improved her health considerably. Now at eleven years old, she managed to squeeze school in and still pick cotton for money to help out—until her beloved grandfather died. Then, shortly after that, Rosa's mother took seriously ill. And soon so did her grandmother.

Now young Rosa took care of everything herself. She took care of the chronically sick women, watched out for her younger brother, Sylvester, cleaned the house, cooked the meals, did many of the farm chores—and she even worked as a maid to bring in cash. Eventually Sylvester was working outside the home too but by the time Rosa was twelve, she was the main breadwinner and caretaker of the house.

Even before these circumstances, Rosa had been a responsible child and a good older sister. But things were dire now, and she stepped up to meet the problem. She accepted that she now needed to give all her time and energy to her home and family. There was no time for school any longer, and she dropped out.

Rosa's faith meant everything to her as she went about her difficult and often lonely teenage years. God was most certainly with her. But there would be no attending school, no high school fun, no hanging out with friends doing nothing. She needed to stay on top of things at home, and she needed to work outside her home. Childhood was over.

If Rosa McCauley could have seen ahead to the future, maybe it could have helped with her struggles. If she could have seen ahead to the future, she'd see that she had a very fulfilling and exciting life ahead of her. And it started when she turned nineteen.

In 1932, Rosa met Raymond Parks. He was immediately taken with Rosa, but she wasn't interested in Raymond, whom everyone called Parks. For one thing, he was very light-complexioned. Given the attitudes she'd grown up with about white people, she didn't even like to be with black people who looked white. She herself was light-complexioned, but Parks was even lighter. When he wore a hat, he could have passed for white if he wanted to, and Rosa did not trust that. She would later realize that she was judging a book by its cover, and that wasn't right. But in the beginning, romance was not on Rosa's mind when it came to Parks.

Parks was ten years older than nineteen-year-old Rosa. He worked as a barber and owned a red car. Owning a car was rare among black men in those parts, and Parks started taking Rosa for car rides. Rosa's mother adored Parks (Grandma had died three years before). So Mother approved of Rosa going in a car with Parks, who found that while driving, he could talk to Rosa and she would talk to him. They discovered they had a great deal in common.

But for Rosa, it was more than having things in common. She was impressed that Parks was doing important civil rights work and actually risking his life to do it. He was involved in the National Association for the Advancement of Colored People (NAACP), and he was working for the benefit of some young black men—known as the Scottsboro Boys—who were railroaded into jail over crimes they did not commit. They had been put on death row. Parks was involved in a secret committee to raise legal funds to help these young men who had been unjustly sentenced, and it was dangerous work if the wrong white people found out. He told Rosa only enough about it so that she would know he was involved but not enough to know who was involved in it with him.

Having grown up with her sense of justice and her righteous anger over things that were wrong, it stands to reason that Rosa thought very highly of Parks. She grew to love his fearlessness and inner strength. For the first time, she shared her thoughts and feelings about being a black woman to someone else. They fell in love and were married before the year was out.

Theirs was a happy marriage, full of love and mutual respect. The first thing Parks insisted was that Rosa go back to school and get her diploma, even though he too had needed to drop out of school to work. So one year after she married, Rosa Parks was also a high school graduate. Few African Americans at the time could say that.

Rosa worked as a tailor at a department store in Montgomery, and Parks continued working as a barber. Rosa's mother lived with them in their small house. The couple enjoyed church together. And they were very active in their local NAACP and other organizations.

The Scottsboro case continued to keep Parks involved, and he and Rosa decided she should not be involved at all. It was dangerous—too dangerous, Parks felt, for Rosa. They agreed that he would not share much about his dealings in the Scottsboro case so that she could honestly say she knew nothing. Sometimes there were threats from the Ku Klux Klan, and Rosa worried about Parks's safety. But eventually the Scottsboro Boys were spared execution. Parks could now turn some of his attention to other things.

Rosa volunteered at NAACP meetings to document the testimony of people who had been badly treated by police or were in jail or had watched someone killed because of race. She stayed calm while doing this, but she was often on the brink of despair at the way of the world. She held on to her faith and kept on working with her local civil rights groups.

In 1955, Rosa was invited to attend a retreat at Highlander Folk School in Tennessee. It was a ten-day workshop called "Racial Desegregation." She wanted to attend but didn't think she could afford it. Then friends in the NAACP offered to pay her way. Parks didn't want to go himself but supported her decision to attend.

Rosa made friends at Highlander, surprisingly most of them white. Rosa had often worked in white people's homes as a maid, and she would later say of Highlander, "One of my greatest pleasures there was enjoying the smell of bacon frying and coffee brewing and knowing that white folks were doing the preparing instead of me." But it was also amazing to her that she was actually talking to and working with white people who treated her just like they treated one another. This was completely new for Rosa, who had avoided white people back home.

As for the Highlander staff, they were impressed with Rosa Parks. And by the end of the year, they'd realize why.

The Civil Rights movement of the United States dealt with a host of issues. It tended to be most effective when a group of people focused on one area of denied rights at a time and worked hard until that thing changed. One such issue was Jim Crow treatment on public transportation.

Many African-American workers in the South could not afford cars to drive. They depended on bus transportation to get them to work or anywhere else that wasn't within walking distance. But taking a bus in the South could be a very unpleasant experience for black passengers—inefficient and potentially humiliating.

Each city bus had a designated number of seats—all in the back—for black passengers. First, black people needed to board through the front door, pay the fare, then turn around and go back outside to board through the back door. If all the seats for whites were full, blacks needed to give up the designated seats for blacks if whites required a seat. If there were empty seats in the white section but the black section was full, then blacks could sit in the white section unless and until a white person boarded and wanted the seat. Then the black passenger needed to give his or her seat to the white passenger.

And blacks and whites could not share a row, even if an aisle ran between the seats. So if a white passenger wanted a seat in the black section because the white section was full, four black passengers would all have to give up their seats. Then that entire row went to the white passenger.

Rosa Parks was one of those people who took the bus and disliked doing it. She walked whenever possible. She was especially annoyed with the situation because, twelve years ago, she had paid her fare, gotten off to reboard in the back, and watched the bus take off without her. She always remembered the driver—James F. Blake. If she saw him in the driver's seat, she would not board the bus.

On December 1, 1955, Rosa Parks left work and boarded a bus for home without noticing Blake was driving. She paid her fare, got off the bus, and boarded through the rear door. She sat down in the first row of the black passenger section on an aisle seat next to a black man. Across the aisle were two black women. All four seats in the row were occupied.

Eventually the bus's white section filled up. The next white passenger was a man who came to Rosa's aisle expecting all four black passengers to stand so that he could sit. The two women got up, but Rosa did not. The bus driver watched in his mirror, and finally said, "I'm going to need those seats, y'all." Rosa realized it was Blake, the driver she tried to avoid.

When the black man next to Rosa stood, she swung her legs around so he could leave, then she slid over to the window seat and remained there. Once people realized she was refusing to stand, the bus went silent.

Blake got up and walked to the back of the bus. "Let me have that seat," he said.

Rosa stayed put, silent.

"Are you going to stand up?"

Rosa looked at the driver and said, "No."

Blake responded, "Then I'm going to have you arrested."

"You may do that," said Rosa.

Nobody made a sound. And nobody left.

Eventually the police arrived and discussed the situation outside. Then they boarded the bus and escorted Rosa Parks off the bus and into their cruiser. They took her to jail where they took her fingerprints and her mug shot. Then they put her in a cell.

Word got out fast around town. The black community was amazed that this middle-aged member of the church choir had just defied Jim Crow law. But the local black activists were ready for this. The civil rights leaders of the city had watched more than one woman refuse to give up her bus seat, and they had been waiting for the "right" person to be a test case for this Jim Crow policy. The year before they had almost used a young high school student, but in the end they decided she wasn't quite right to be the symbol they needed, though they certainly appreciated her actions.

Rosa Parks, however, was perfect to be the face of the movement. And what a serene face it was.

From jail, Rosa asked for her one phone call and was ignored. For quite a while, nobody would speak to her at all, but they finally allowed her phone call. Her husband collected bail money from donations, hired an attorney, and hurried to the police station. Fortunately Rosa did not have to spend the night in jail. She went home, exhausted.

But Montgomery's civil rights activists worked all night. They had the perfect person to be the symbol of what Jim Crow did to people. They got out thirty-five thousand fliers calling for black people to mobilize. Here's what the fliers said:

This is for Monday, December 5, 1955

Another Negro woman has been arrested and thrown into jail because she refused to get up out of her seat on the bus and give it to a white person.

It is the second time since the Claudette Colvin case that a Negro woman has been arrested for the same thing. This has to be stopped.

Negroes have rights, too, for if Negroes did not ride the buses, they could not operate. Three-fourths of the riders are Negroes, yet we are arrested, or have to stand over empty seats. If we do not do something to stop these arrests, they will continue. The next time it may be you, or your daughter, or mother.

This woman's case will come up on Monday. We are, therefore, asking every Negro to stay off the buses Monday in protest of the arrest and trial. Don't ride the buses to work, to town, to school, or anywhere on Monday.

You can afford to stay out of school for one day. If you work, take a cab or walk. But please, children and grown-ups, don't ride the bus at all on Monday. Please stay off all buses Monday.

Monday came and not one black person stepped foot on a bus in Montgomery. They walked, they pooled money for taxis, they did whatever they needed to do to get to work. If they were teenagers, they piled as many as they could into one car and drove to school. Rosa, however, went to court that day.

When Rosa headed into the courthouse for her sentencing, there was a crowd of black people outside to support her. Rosa was dressed primly with a small tasteful hat. One teenage girl with a high voice called out, "Oh she's so sweet! They've messed with the wrong one now!" It became a chant for the crowd. "They've messed with the wrong one now!" they shouted in unison.

And indeed they had messed with the wrong one. Rosa Parks was without reproach. She was a hardworking woman, was married to a respectable man, was caring for her ailing mother, was a member of the church choir, had never before been arrested or in any trouble whatsoever—and was willing to take on the fight. As she put it, "The white people couldn't point to me and say that there was anything I had done to deserve such treatment except to be born black."

The judge found her guilty and imposed a fine, which she never paid. The fact that he convicted her meant the attorneys could now take it to a higher court, which was their intention.

That night there was a gathering at Holt Baptist Church led by a young minister named Dr. Martin Luther King Jr., someone Rosa had never met or heard of. By the time the service was over, a list of demands had been drawn up to give to the bus company and to Montgomery's civic leaders. Rosa Parks had a new friend too—Dr. King. The two remained friends until his death.

The demands were delivered and ignored. The bus boycott continued. After a few weeks, many black maids and babysitters had a new means of transportation—the white ladies they worked for, who were not going to live without their help nor put up with tardiness. So they became chauffeurs for the women who worked for them. All around Montgomery one could see white ladies driving cars with one or more black ladies in the backseat.

The boycott lasted 381 days, and it did what it was intended to do—it nearly broke the bus companies for lack of business and it resulted in the desegregation of the Montgomery bus system.

But Rosa and Parks paid dearly. Both of them lost their jobs over the boycott, and they were unable to find new ones in Montgomery. They also suffered death threats even after the boycott was over. Rosa's brother, Sylvester, was living in Detroit and loving it. He invited his family to come on up and start over. He even sent money for the trip.

In 1957, Rosa, Parks, and Rosa's mother all moved north to Detroit, Michigan. Parks got his Michigan barber's license and could work again. Rosa eventually worked in the office of attorney John Conyers, who would become a longtime federal congressman. Rosa worked for Conyers for twenty-three years, and she continued her activities in civil rights on a more limited level as she got older. She spoke at the March on Washington with Dr. King and at a few other events. The two continued to be fans of one another. When Dr. King was assassinated, Rosa was so devastated she cried for days, constantly saying aloud the twenty-seventh Psalm for comfort.

Life in Detroit was not bad until the 1970s, when it became difficult for Rosa as within a two-year period Parks, Sylvester, and her mother all died. Rosa and Parks never had children, but she still had Sylvester's children around her. She retired from her work with Conyers. She continued making occasional appearances, and she authored books about her life.

In 2005, Rosa Parks died in Detroit at the age of ninety-two. In both Montgomery and Detroit, the front seats of city buses were reserved with black ribbons in honor of Rosa Parks for the days between her death and her funeral. Her body was flown to Montgomery, where she lay in repose at the St. Paul AME Church. After the memorial service there, her body was flown to Washington, DC, to lie in state at the Capitol Rotunda. She was the first woman and the second African American to lie in state at the Capitol. Then her body was flown back to Detroit where, after a long funeral full of speeches by notables, a horse-drawn hearse carried her to the cemetery. As the hearse passed through the city, thousands lined the streets to applaud for this dignified woman who did so much for civil rights.

Rosa Parks was a quiet heroine. About her famous sit-down moment that would change history, she remarked, "People always say that I didn't give up my seat because I was tired, but that isn't true. I was not tired physically, or no more tired than I usually was at the end of a working day. . . . No, the only tired I was, was tired of giving in."

Today she is mostly known for that one moment of defying racism on a city bus. The truth is that she was a fighter before that event and she was a fighter after—but always in peace and with the love of Christ in her heart.

● Think...

1. Along with simply being African-American, there were many things that contributed to Rosa's growing up acutely aware of injustice. What were some contributing factors in her life and background?

2. In what city and state did Rosa's refusal to give up her seat spark a protest?

3. Why did Rosa and her family move to Detroit?

◆ Imagine...

What do you feel strongly about? Would you go to jail in protest over it? What are some circumstances in which that could happen? Why is this thing so important to you?

■ Get Creative!

That thing you might go to jail over . . . write a monologue—a piece that's meant to be spoken aloud by one person—about being in jail and what your thoughts are while there. Explore in your monologue more personal things you might feel while in jail: fears for your safety, your reputation, your faith, your worried family, and so on. If possible, perform your monologue for your class or another group.

11

Fannie Lou Hamer

(1917–1977)

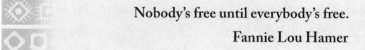

Nobody's free until everybody's free.

Fannie Lou Hamer

On a blistering hot day in Mississippi, a little girl picked cotton. She sang songs while she picked—spirituals, folk tunes, hymns from church, anything she knew by heart. At only six years of age, this black child—one of twenty children in her family—worked right alongside the older kids and grown-ups in the cotton fields, and like them she earned wages to help support her family.

She would be known for this spirited hymn-singing all her life.

She also would be known for her unusual courage.

Fannie Lou Townsend was born in 1917, the youngest of six girls and fourteen boys, all grandchildren of a slave. Of course by now slavery was long over, and Fannie Lou and her family were technically free Americans. But there was very little "free" about being an African American in Mississippi in the first half of the twentieth century.

The large Townsend family lived in a tiny house on someone else's land—a huge farm, still called a "plantation" just like it had been called before the Civil War so many years ago. The Townsend children all stepped up to help their parents eke out a living on this plantation as sharecroppers. This meant they farmed the white owner's land, and then at harvesttime any profits from the crops were split in half with the landowner who did not actually work that land. Farming was a tough way to earn a living—so much depended on weather and other conditions that would impact the price of crops at harvest. Some years, there wasn't even enough food for the Townsend table.

As a child, Fannie Lou was often hungry and not properly clothed. Her mother wrapped her children's feet in rags because she and her husband could not afford shoes for them. Little Fannie Lou found herself wishing she were white so she and her siblings could eat regularly and live easier. She would eventually learn that it wasn't about being white; it was about being fair. Fannie Lou would grow up and decide to do something about these wrongs.

But that was later on. At age six, Fannie Lou contracted the dreaded disease of polio. In spite of no money and little medical help, she managed to heal better than most, though she walked with a limp for the rest of her life. She was able to go back to school and back to picking cotton when she wasn't in school.

And Fannie Lou loved school. She was an excellent student with good grades. She could read and write very well. This was not the case for the average African American in the South at the time, adult or child. Many could not read and write because they never went to school, had to miss too many days of school to work, or had to drop out because of extreme poverty. By the time Fannie Lou was twelve, she too had to drop out of school so she could work in the fields full-time and help support the Townsend family. The nation's laws that kept children in school and provided them with buildings and teachers applied only to white children.

Fannie Lou was glad she was able to stick with school as long as she did, but now she was a full-time fieldworker—that's just how things were. She was a fast worker with a positive spirit, and by the time she turned thirteen, she was picking cotton alongside her older siblings, sometimes two hundred to three hundred pounds of it per day, more than some adults. Cotton on its plant is lightweight; it takes a lot of picking to fill a bag that will weigh three hundred pounds.

As always, young Fannie Lou sang while she worked. Her favorite song was "This Little Light of Mine," a cheerful song to sing in the hot sun. Singing helped the time go by and cheered little Fannie Lou's soul. It cheered other workers, too, when they joined in singing with her. In the years to come, "This Little Light of Mine" would become Fannie Lou's personal anthem.

Young Fannie Lou was such a hard worker that she stood out to the owner of the plantation. He soon realized how smart she was, so he pulled her indoors to work on his accounting books instead of picking cotton. He left it to Fannie Lou to make certain he wasn't being cheated when he sold the harvest. She missed the singing and being with the other workers, but she enjoyed using her mind. She liked the challenge of taking care of the books.

As Fannie Lou grew to become a young woman, it looked like life would be fairly typical for her in her time and place in society. She continued working in and around the cotton fields. She married another sharecropper, a well-respected man by the name of Perry Hamer whom everyone called "Pap." When Fannie Lou learned she was unable to bear children, she and Pap adopted a daughter whom they loved very much. This daughter would marry and give them grandchildren—children Fannie Lou and Pap would eventually raise themselves when their daughter's health failed.

The Hamer family lived in a small house on the cotton plantation they worked in Ruleville, Mississippi. They owned their house, though it sat on the plantation so they didn't own the land the house sat on. But they got by for years—until things changed. When Fannie Lou reached middle age, her life turned out to be far different than she or anyone else would imagine. What chance did little Fannie Lou Townsend, fieldworker and school dropout, have of breaking out of poverty and racism to make a change that affected millions? Little to none. And yet she would do just that. Life in the Mississippi delta would no longer be average for Mrs. Fannie Lou Hamer.

In the 1950s, the Civil Rights movement for African Americans was gaining momentum in the South. This was a movement to make changes that would give African Americans the full rights of citizenship. They were already citizens, of course, and they legally had the right to vote. But those rights didn't play out like they should, especially in the South. Local governments found all kinds of ways to keep blacks from voting.

It is called civil disobedience, when people use creative ways to call attention to something in society that isn't right. Thanks to the Civil Rights movement, newspapers and nightly television showed the world the desperate conditions and humiliations Southern black people lived with every day. The media also showed the movement fighting the system with speeches, protests, sit-down strikes, and marches.

The American Constitution guarantees certain rights and liberties to all its citizens. But that simply did not hold true in the South among African Americans. They were not treated as citizens. They did not have the right to go wherever they pleased, ride public transportation without certain rules applied only to them, eat in restaurants where white people ate—the list went on and on.

This was segregation—when a group of people is separated to live differently because of race. In the South that segregated system was nicknamed Jim Crow. When civil rights workers used civil disobedience, they spotlighted what was wrong and let it be known that this must change. So civil rights protestors addressed Jim Crow laws and segregation for several years in the

1950s, and many of the attempts for change were successful. Many attempts were not successful. Most were peaceful. Some were not.

In some cases people were injured and sometimes even killed trying to gain their civil rights during those years. This movement of civil disobedience started with educated and influential people. By the time 1960 rolled around, the movement also included poor blacks who had no influence. But they had inner strength. And they had faith in God.

One of those rights of Americans that was flat-out denied to African Americans in the South was their right to vote. White officials used a variety of ways to keep blacks from even registering to vote. Why? Because those officials knew that, should enough African Americans vote in elections, they'd vote to change how things were. They'd vote against Jim Crow. So blacks were blocked at every opportunity. Sometimes in order to attempt to register, black citizens were required to take literacy tests to show they could read or take difficult tests about the Constitution, which they regularly failed. Whites were not required to take such tests.

A movement grew to register African-American voters in the South so that they could vote in elections. That movement came to Ruleville, Mississippi, and that was when Fannie Lou Hamer, age forty-five, tried to register to vote in the Montgomery County courthouse and was refused. One of the times she tried she was given a literacy test, and the very intelligent Fannie Lou was told she'd failed it. She knew she had not failed it. She returned many times to attempt to register to vote and was either refused or told she failed a test. But she determined that she would return every month to the county courthouse until she was able to register.

In June 1963, Fannie Lou attended a voter registration workshop out of town with some other Ruleville people. They traveled by bus, and on the way home they stopped to get something to eat. State patrolmen showed up at the restaurant and arrested Fannie Lou and the others for no known reason. While Fannie Lou was told she was under arrest, the policeman dealing with her actually kicked her.

The Ruleville people were taken to a jail in Montgomery County and put in cells in a full and noisy jailhouse. As soon as Fannie Lou's jail door shut, she became very alarmed because she could hear the sounds of people being beaten. She heard screams and racist name-calling. She heard one woman being interrogated and yelled at and beaten badly, until that woman began praying aloud that God would have mercy on these men who were doing her harm. They continued to beat her.

Fannie Lou was next. She prayed silently for strength as she was carried into another cell by several white men. One of them said to her, "We're going to make you wish you were dead."

The white officers ordered her to lie facedown on a cot. Then a man began to beat her with a hard, leather-covered baton. The jail officers held her down as the man delivered severe and painful blows. Fannie Lou attempted to protect the side of her body that had been injured by polio, but she was unable to move. The man who beat her was finally exhausted, so a second man stepped up to continue the beating. Then the officers beat her on and around her head. All this time they yelled at her and called her humiliating names.

In the end, Fannie Lou was released from jail to go home. She was very injured, and she suffered the physical effects of the beating for the rest of her life. Her kidney was permanently damaged, and she lost her sight in one eye. She nearly lost her life in this jailhouse beating at the hands of the people paid to protect and serve.

But she did not give in to fear. Fannie Lou was undeterred even by this violence. She believed in her right to vote as an American. Now she became a fearless and plainspoken champion of the right for all African Americans to vote. She focused on that. She believed the fight was not simply a legal one; she believed it was a righteous struggle that was blessed by God. Then while she worked tirelessly toward voter registration, Fannie Lou finally was told she had passed the tests she'd had to take at the courthouse. She registered to vote in 1963. On that day, out of almost half a million Mississippi African

Americans eligible to be voters, she was one of only twenty-eight thousand of them registered to vote.

But trouble wasn't over. This act of registering to vote got Fannie Lou into trouble that very day. When she returned home from the courthouse, her family told her they were being evicted. The white owner of the plantation showed up again, very angry because he found out Fannie Lou had registered. So he claimed the Hamers owed him money, which they did not, since they owned their house. He offered to forgive the debt and allow everyone to stay put if Fannie Lou would go back to the courthouse and withdraw her registration. He explained to her that Mississippi was not ready for such things as black people voting.

Fannie Lou pulled herself up as straight as she could at five feet four inches and faced the plantation owner. "I did not register for you," she said. "I registered for myself." She refused to withdraw her registration, so the Hamers were forced to leave their home that very night. They also immediately lost their jobs. After they left their home, the Ku Klux Klan shot up the houses of people involved in the Hamers' lives in Ruleville.

Obviously this was dangerous living for Fannie Lou, first with the beating and now with the threat of the Klan. But she continued to work fearlessly. "Nobody's free until everybody's free," she said. As a registered voter, Fannie Lou Hamer cast her votes in every election, and she even ran for Congress in Mississippi. She did not win, and she knew she would not win, because only a fraction of black Mississippians were registered to vote. But she knew her candidacy would spotlight the issue of voter registration.

In 1964, Fannie Lou joined volunteers from all over the nation who converged in Mississippi, many of them college students, in what became known as Freedom Summer. This was a Mississippi movement to register black voters. The Freedom Summer team members covered the state trying to get other African Americans to register to vote. They also provided schooling for African Americans so that they could learn to read, a valuable skill any time and a necessary one for voting in Mississippi at the time.

Among the young voter registration workers, Fannie Lou became known as "the lady who sings the hymns." The little girl who sang while she picked cotton in the fields, who lifted up the spirits of her co-workers, now inspired a younger generation by singing songs on their bus rides like "This Little Light of Mine," "Wade in the Water," "Walk with Me, Lord," and "Go Tell It on the Mountain." Sometimes they would all make up new verses to go with these songs to keep them focused on their goals. Audio recordings of Fannie Lou Hamer singing in her deep and confident voice are very powerful even today.

That same year, Fannie Lou Hamer also helped found an organization known as the Mississippi Freedom Democratic Party. This organization, made up of both black and white citizens, was intended to draw attention to the fact that all the Democratic Party delegates in Mississippi were not only white (as were all the Republicans) but were not truly representing their constituents. In other words, the elected officials oppressed black citizens as a matter of course by blocking their ability to vote.

That year, the Democratic Party had its presidential convention in Atlantic City, New Jersey. President Lyndon Baines Johnson was running for his second term. The convention officials had been approached by civil rights workers to allow delegates from the Mississippi Freedom Democratic Party to join the convention and be seated on behalf of black citizens unable to vote in the state of Mississippi. This caused quite a buzz at the convention and in the White House. After much discussion among convention officials, it was decided that the Freedom Democratic Party would be allowed to give testimony to the convention about why they should be given seats in the convention.

The first speaker was Fannie Lou Hamer. In film footage, this short, middle-aged woman, dressed in a simple cotton print dress and carrying her purse on her elbow, approached the microphone. She held her head high and displayed no nervousness, even though she was about to speak to a huge roomful of hundreds of white people and to television microphones and cameras for the first time in her life.

All those years of singing in fields had given Fannie Lou a commanding voice. She addressed the officials and said: "My name is Mrs. Fannie Lou Hamer and I live at 626 East Lafayette Street in Ruleville, Mississippi, Sunflower County," and she went on to name her area senators. This beginning to her speech may seem ordinary, but it was in itself a courageous thing for a black woman from Mississippi to do because she told the world—and the Klan and any corrupt lawmakers—how to find her. It also highlighted the names of some senators who were not supporting their black citizens.

Fannie Lou then told the convention members the story of her attempts to register to vote. She gave details about her arrest and her subsequent beating. There was silence in that cavernous room as she told her truth. In eight minutes of calm, clear speech and detailed reporting, this Mississippi fieldworker stunned the listeners. And soon the world. To this day, her speech stands as one of the most famous and powerful speeches in the American cause for civil rights.

President Johnson started watching the live television broadcast, and within a few minutes, he ordered the networks to break away from Fannie Lou. He saw a threat to his election chances in this down-to-earth, clear-speaking woman's compelling testimony of being severely beaten by officials, and he didn't want any controversy to mar his campaign. For some reason the president feared the effect of this fieldworker on her listeners more than he feared the effect of the ever-present Dr. Martin Luther King Jr. Johnson stopped the live broadcasting mid-speech, supposedly to give an emergency press conference.

Nevertheless, the networks played the speech in its entirety later that night, so the world did hear Fannie Lou's horrific story. They heard her sum up the situation in simple language. "All this was because we wanted to register, to become first-class citizens." Then they heard her conclude, "I question America. Is this America, the land of the free and the home of the brave?"

This presentation itself caused quite a stir. And it helped to start change in the obstacles to voting. The following year Congress passed the Voting Rights Act, and President Johnson signed it into law. This assured that African

Americans would have their right to vote without obstacles such as written tests for registration or having to pay an extra tax in order to cast a vote. The numbers of black people becoming voters rose instantly because of this.

Fannie Lou Hamer never stopped working for civil rights. Yes, southern blacks had the vote, but there were so many other problems that still needed addressing—poverty, illiteracy, hunger. She never forgot her misplaced childhood wish to be white because she was hungry and her feet were cold. She did not want any other children to live that way or to wish they were someone else because of it.

By 1974, the still dedicated and hardworking Fannie Lou began having health problems. That didn't stop her from traveling and speaking to fund the movements that would improve the lives of black Americans. Back home, she personally fed those in need in her own house, clothed them, and paid their bills from her fund-raising tours or her personal account. By now, her husband had concerns for his wife's health, and he felt people took advantage of her kindness. While he was most likely correct, he also knew this was who his wife was, and he'd best not try to stop her.

In 1977 Fannie Lou Hamer died from heart failure at only age fifty-nine. She did not live a long life, but what an impact this woman had on her world. She was honored in a full-house memorial service in her church and an overflow service in the local high school with an attendance of over 1,500 people. She was buried in her hometown of Ruleville, Mississippi, where her gravestone carries an engraved sentence she was known to say, something that most certainly propelled her forward toward her goals: "I am sick and tired of being sick and tired."

Mrs. Fannie Lou Hamer had truly let her light shine.

● Think…

1. Why did Fannie have to drop out of school?

2. Where was Fannie when she was arrested and put in jail?

3. Explain why Fannie and her colleagues wanted to be seated at the Democratic Convention.

◆ Imagine…

After Fannie went through her frightening ordeal in jail and sustained lifelong injuries from it, how do you think she was able to go on with the movement? How did she keep from hating her captors? Do you think you could do the same or not? Write down your thoughts on this and discuss with others if you can.

● Get Creative!

In Fannie's famous speech before the Democratic convention, she states the names of her senators. Find the names of the senators representing your area, and write one of them a letter. If you feel strongly that something needs changing, let him or her know—respectfully, of course. If you think he or she is doing a good job of representing your area, be sure to say that.

12

Althea Gibson

(1927–2003)

 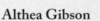 No matter what accomplishments you make, somebody helped you.

Althea Gibson

It was Harlem, the famous neighborhood at the north end of New York City, and in the late 1930s Harlem was a lively place. It hopped day and night. Everywhere people were on sidewalks, walking to and from whatever work they could find during the Great Depression, to and from church and school, or to and from whatever mischief they could get into in this tightly populated area.

Usually there was music playing somewhere that could be heard on the sidewalk. The smells of home cooking wafted out of tenements or from corner pushcarts. Men sold fresh vegetables from horse-drawn wagons. Kids played hopscotch on the sidewalks or played catch in the street. An occasional automobile, still a fairly rare thing to own, rolled down the streets, horn honking to move kids and stray dogs out of the way.

People worked hard in Harlem—when they could find work—then came home to perch on the front stoops and socialize with each other. Everyone knew everyone's business because, even though Harlem was next to busy Manhattan, it was more like a small town for the African Americans who lived there.

Smack-dab in the middle of Harlem lived a young, leggy black girl with a huge smile. She was the kind of girl people called a tomboy because she wasn't one to play with dolls. This girl loved to play anything competitive and athletic on the sidewalks or in the streets, mostly with the boys. She was fun and energetic—and she was good at any sport she touched.

But school was tough for her. She didn't understand a lot of the lessons. She struggled even to pay attention to the teacher, fighting the urge to simply stare out the window—or bolt out the door. Some days she just felt too jumpy to be there, and she'd stay away from school for a while.

At home, she was the oldest of five kids in the family apartment. Their father had a bad temper, which he often turned on his oldest child. He was even known to beat her. So the girl stayed away from home as much as she could. It seemed like the more she stayed away, the stricter her father became, and then the more she stayed away. Many times neighbors saw the child's long legs sprinting down the stoop, up the street, and into the crowds of people, her angry father calling after her.

Staying away from home so much made the girl get into more mischief than she should have. And staying away from school so much caused her to get behind in her studies.

But during these tough days, she learned to play paddleball. She loved to compete, and she was so good at paddleball that she became almost unbeatable in the neighborhood. By the time she was ten, she had won so many paddleball tournaments in the neighborhood that adult spectators started talking to each other about her. Since this child was so good at this sport, what would she be like at tennis? It took the same kind of skills. She ought to play tennis. But that took money.

So spectators and neighbors in the community took up a collection for the long-legged girl. And the rest would be history.

Althea Neale Gibson was born on a hot August day in 1927 in rural South Carolina in Clarendon County, the first child born to sharecroppers Annie Bell Gibson and Daniel Gibson. Within a couple of years, the Great Depression would devastate America's economy, and consequently in 1930, Althea's family moved north to find better work.

They landed in New York City's Harlem neighborhood on 143rd Street. The move did not much improve the family finances, but it did get the folks out of the cotton fields. Up north, work was hard to come by and money was tight. The Gibsons eventually went on welfare in order to feed their five kids.

Fortunately home was near an area in Harlem where streets were blocked off and called a designated play area. The city hoped to keep children out of trouble and focused on a goal by giving them a place to stretch their limbs and play. Althea had a lot of physical energy and undiscovered talent but very little focus for a long time. Her father taught her how to box, an unusual thing for a father to teach his daughter in those days, and she was pretty good at it, as she would be most sports. But she did not really have an interest in boxing.

Althea's father was strict and sometimes even beat her. To avoid these confrontations, Althea for many years would just stay away from home as much as possible. She also stayed away from school so much that she would drop out in the eighth grade.

When she was ten years old, she was a constant presence in those Harlem "play areas." In 1940, the community sponsored paddleball competitions, which Althea loved to play. After three years, she won so many times that her neighborhood pooled money to get her into the Cosmopolitan Tennis Club where she could use her paddleball skills to learn tennis. It would also help smooth Althea's rough edges in her personality and provide her with some social skills.

The plan was successful, and Althea first became a competent and then an impressive tennis player. At a lean and muscular five feet eleven inches, she was all arms and legs—but at the same time graceful and powerful. A prominent South Carolina couple decided to invest in her. They invited her to live with them and finish school while taking private tennis lessons. Althea never forgot the many people who believed in her. "I always wanted to be somebody," she said. "If I made it, it's half because I was game enough to take a lot of punishment along the way and half because there were a lot of people who cared enough to help me."

By now, the decade was the fifties, and racial bigotry was alive and well all over America. Tennis was played mostly by white people, in particular those white people who could afford leisure time. Some black people did play tennis, but they were never allowed to play in private tennis clubs. They played on public courts only. When it came to competition, tennis was absolutely an all-white sport and it seemed committed to staying that way.

Althea competed in the American Tennis Association (ATA) tournaments, winning all but one of them from 1944 through 1956. Nevertheless, she could not compete in the bigger competitions—only because she was black. In particular, she was shut out from entering the US Nationals. She tried to get in but was unsuccessful.

It took a four-time US Nationals champion tennis player named Alice Marble, a white woman, to help things change. In 1950, she wrote an article in the magazine *American Lawn Tennis* and told readers that the phenomenal Althea Gibson was not allowed to participate in bigger tournaments for only one reason: bigotry. She wrote, "If Althea Gibson represents a challenge to the present crop of players, then it's only fair that they meet this challenge on the courts." In other words, she challenged the tennis community to bring it on and play with Althea Gibson—unless they really were that racist.

It worked. Althea appeared at the US Nationals in Forest Hills, New York, in 1950, the first African American, male or female, to enter the competition. In 1951, she was the first black tennis player to compete at Wimbledon. By March 1953, she was rated seventh out of the top ten tennis players in the United States.

During this time, Althea also went to college. She graduated and received her degree from Florida A&M University in 1953 and became an athletic instructor at Lincoln University in Missouri.

When Althea competed at Wimbledon again in 1957, she won the singles division. The press had a field day, noting that she had not only broken the color barrier at Wimbledon but was stunning to watch play with her long limbs, graceful reach, and intimidating serve. The *New York Times* said, "Miss Gibson was in rare form . . . she became the first member of her race to rule the world of tennis."

She also competed in doubles that year at Wimbledon. Getting a partner for doubles had been a problem at first. It seemed white American tennis players didn't want to pair with her. But she found a partner in British player Angela Buxton from Liverpool, England. Angela shook her head at the fact that America ignored Althea because she was black, and England ignored Angela because she was Jewish. So having that experience in common, they decided it was a good pairing, and they in fact made great tennis partners— they won the doubles. Best of all, Althea and Angela would remain friends for life.

At Wimbledon, Althea received her award from Queen Elizabeth. Althea later said, "Shaking hands with the Queen of England was a long way from being forced to sit in the colored section of the bus going into downtown Wilmington, North Carolina." Althea was the first black tennis player to win Wimbledon, and it would be 1975 before an African American would win Wimbledon again. That would be Arthur Ashe.

The victorious Althea Gibson returned home to a ticker tape parade down Broadway in New York City. She was only the second African American to be given that honor. Estimates say that 100,000 people lined the streets to honor her.

The following year, 1958, she won the US Open, the first African American woman to do so. She now became the first black woman on the covers of both *Time* and *Sports Illustrated*, and the Associated Press named her Female Athlete of the Year.

If we pause to think about how a child who quit school in the eighth grade and suffered poverty, parental abuse, and racial injustice had the kind of spirit that wins, we can learn what we need to know by reading Althea's own words. She said, "I knew that I was an unusual, talented girl, through the grace of God. I didn't need to prove that to myself. I only wanted to prove it to my opponents."

If we pause to think how this African-American woman could chalk up so many "firsts" in a predominantly white sport when the racial climate at the time was so difficult, again, we go to Althea's own words. "The loser is always part of the problem; the winner is always part of the answer. The loser always has an excuse; the winner always has a program. The loser says it may be possible, but it's difficult; the winner says it may be difficult, but it's possible."

Having that kind of confidence, it's no wonder that by the end of 1958 Althea had won Wimbledon, the US Open, and eleven Grand Slam titles around the globe.

In the 1950s, there was no prize money for amateur athletes. Being a competing athlete in tennis did not pay like it does today. Althea also did not receive offers to do endorsements like other players did, and that was most likely due to race.

To make a living, Althea played in exhibition shows, often opening on tour for the highly entertaining basketball team, the Harlem Globetrotters. She said, "Being champion is all well and good, but you can't eat a crown."

So in 1958, she retired from tennis.

Always a little restless, Althea now tried her hand at playing golf. She found she loved golf, and she excelled at it. She became the first black woman to play the professional golf circuit, and she even made a living doing it.

Once again, she was playing a sport whose participants at the time were still mostly white. When Althea was thirty-seven years old, she began touring and playing golf with the Ladies Professional Golf Association. The biggest shock for her was how strong racism still was in the South even in the midsixties. She was a famous American who had been honored all over the world. Nevertheless, a country club in Texas decided they would let her play on the golf course but not allow her to use either the clubhouse or the restroom. Althea dressed in her car.

Over the years, Althea would dabble in a number of things. She had always been an accomplished singer, so she recorded an album of music. She was also a fine saxophone player. She wrote her autobiography, published in 1958, titled *I Always Wanted to Be Somebody*. She even acted in one movie—a 1959 John Wayne movie called *The Horse Soldiers*. Eventually she was appointed the athletic commissioner in New Jersey, though she didn't remain in that position for long.

The awards rolled in, and here are only some of them: in 1971, she was inducted into the National Lawn Tennis Hall of Fame and also into the International Tennis Hall of Fame. In 1974, she was inducted into the Black Athletes Hall of Fame. In 1983, she was inducted into the South Carolina Hall of Fame and the following year into the Florida Sports Hall of Fame. In 2002, she was pictured on the front of a Wheaties box as part of a Black History Month series.

Althea continued to take on various projects and try to find ways to earn a living. Then in 1990 she had a stroke, and then another stroke. Within a couple of years, she was housebound and struggling physically, financially, and emotionally.

The stroke most likely changed her personality, and Althea became very depressed. She reached out in desperation to her former doubles partner and longtime friend, Angela Buxton. Greatly alarmed, Buxton spearheaded a drive to get people in the tennis community to donate money for Althea's health care and well-being. Buxton raised over a million dollars, and that helped ease the stress of Althea's final years considerably.

The world of tennis now had newcomers Venus and Serena Williams. When the sisters were honored at an Althea Gibson Foundation dinner that raised money for scholarships, they were thrilled at a message from Althea herself, through a spokeswoman. Althea congratulated them and called them two of the best tennis players in the world.

Althea made it to her seventy-sixth birthday, but a month later, on September 28, 2003, she died of respiratory failure in East Orange, New Jersey. She had no children. But she left a legacy that endures to this day.

One thing we can thank her for is how she opened doors for other athletes of color. Venus Williams said it well. "I am honored to have followed in such great footsteps. Her accomplishments set the stage for my success, and through players like myself and Serena and many others to come, her legacy will live on."

Althea Gibson had a glorious talent for playing tennis. She had other talents for so many other things, but the world knows her primarily for tennis. She knew she had a God-given gift, and she only wished to play it out. Anyone who saw her play tennis never forgot what they saw.

In the movie *Chariots of Fire*, one of the Olympic runners acknowledges that he knows it was God who made him fast. So whenever the man runs, he could feel the pleasure of the Lord. Perhaps Althea knew this feeling when she played tennis, knowing she was doing what she was so good at, as she said, "through the grace of God."

Toward the end of her life, Althea said, "I want the public to remember me as they knew me: athletic, smart, and healthy . . . remember me strong and tough and quick, fleet of foot and tenacious."

They do, Miss Althea Gibson. They always will.

Think…

1. What sport was Althea playing in Harlem when her neighbors decided to invest in her future?

2. What did Althea and Angela Buxton, her British doubles partner at Wimbledon, feel they had in common?

3. In what new ways did Althea experience racism after she became a pro golfer?

Imagine…

Althea wrote her autobiography and called it *I Always Wanted to Be Somebody*. What might you title your own autobiography?

Get Creative!

Althea wrote about how she wanted to be remembered after she died. Celebrities often think this way, but we can too. Write a paragraph about how you would like to be remembered at this point in your life.

13

Coretta Scott King

(1927–2006)

Hate is too great a burden to bear. It injures the hater more than it injures the hated.

Coretta Scott King

It was Sunday morning in rural Alabama. The sun was a low orange ball as the family walked to church. Church time was a favorite time for the child and her family. There were many reasons for that, but mostly for the child, it was the music.

Living in the throes of the Great Depression, the family wasn't destitute but they had no money for extras either. So to be at church with a piano and to hear the hymns sung in four vocal parts was exciting for the little girl. She was learning to read music out of the hymnbook, too, and even that was a fun challenge for her eager mind. She was a quiet child until it was time to sing, and then she opened up and sang, happy and no longer quiet.

Mommy said she would make sure her quiet little girl got an education, even though she herself didn't have one. She promised the little girl that Mommy would own only one dress if that's what had to happen to get all the money pulled together, but her daughter was going to college.

To be a singer! the little girl added silently.

As the little girl grew up, Mommy did what she said she would do—she made sure her daughter got an education. Now she was on her way to becoming a professional concert singer.

But something happened that rerouted her hopes and dreams in a completely different direction—an important direction, one that was exciting and heartbreaking all at the same time. And the little-girl-turned-woman never looked back.

Coretta Scott was born April 27, 1927, to Bernice (McMurray) and Obadiah Scott in Heiberger, Alabama, not far from the town of Marion. She was born at home. Her mother was assisted in childbirth by Coretta's grandmother, a midwife and former slave. Coretta was the third of four children. Only three survived childhood, thereby making Coretta the baby of the family.

Her parents farmed land that the family had owned since the end of the Civil War. This was unusual for the time. Coretta grew up on this farm with the sense of slavery being not so long ago, but more importantly, she grew up with exceptionally strong and resourceful adults who rose well above slavery's legacy.

Although they were landowners, the family was not well off by any means. It was the Great Depression, when basic life essentials—food, housing, other necessities—were hard to afford. Thanks to the farm, the Scott family always had food on the table. But Coretta and her sister Edythe and brother Obie picked cotton to earn money for the household.

I'm fulfilled in what I do. I never
thought that a lot of money or
fine clothes—the finer things
of life—would make you happy.
My concept of happiness is to
be filled in a spiritual sense.

—*Coretta Scott King*

Both parents had strong personalities and creative minds. They were people who found solutions where others might see only insurmountable problems. Daddy Obadiah Scott was a smart and likable man with a warm personality. He farmed his own land, and he was the first African American in the area to own a truck. But he was always interested in being in business for himself, so he also eventually opened a general store and gas station and was successful at it. He also expanded from one truck into a trucking business.

Mother Bernice Scott was a somewhat shy and beautiful woman with high cheekbones and straight black hair—an appearance that Coretta's features would echo. Mrs. Scott had had very little education but was fiercely determined her children would graduate from high school and even go to college. It would not be easy, but she would help make that happen.

Since school was nine miles away, Mrs. Scott solved the distance problem herself. She actually bought a bus, learned to drive it, and drove her children to school. Other children were welcome to get on board and come along too. Again, this was in the Great Depression, when resources were not easily available. To see a southern black woman take matters into her own hands and find such a solution—it was unique for the time and place. But Mrs. Scott somehow managed it. She had decided what was important and what was not, and she informed Coretta that she was going to college even if her mother "didn't have but one dress to put on."

Mother Bernice had her day. Daughter Coretta graduated as valedictorian from her high school, class of 1945. She went on to Antioch College in Ohio, where she received her Bachelor of Arts degree in music and education in 1951. She then attended the New England Conservatory of Music in Boston and earned a degree in voice and violin in 1953.

Music was a natural direction for Coretta. All of the family liked to sing in church. They sang hymns, and Coretta was often given solos. In high school, her singing interests widened into singing classical music, and that's when she decided to become a concert vocalist. Coretta had turned into a beautiful young woman with a fine soprano voice. After she received her degree at Antioch, she was offered a scholarship to attend the conservatory in Boston. She felt tremendous fulfillment studying music, and while in Boston, she had occasional opportunities to sing publicly.

It was when Coretta studied at the conservatory that she met her future husband. Her friend Mary Powell knew a young man named Martin Luther King Jr. He was a graduate student at Boston University. He told Mary Powell that he was looking for a wife and had become rather "cynical" in his dating life. He asked Mary if she knew any "nice, attractive young ladies" he could meet. She talked about Coretta and gave him her phone number.

Coretta and Martin first met on the phone. He told her, "This is M. L. King Jr. A mutual friend of ours told me about you and gave me your telephone number. She said some very wonderful things about you, and I'd like very much to meet you and talk to you." Then they talked about all kinds of things—music and "racial and economic injustice and the question of peace." He was surprised to learn that she had been somewhat involved in the movement for racial equality. He asked to meet in person and have lunch, and she agreed.

Once they met, Martin would report later in his autobiography, "After an hour, my mind was made up. I said, 'So you can do something else besides sing? You've got a good mind also. You have everything I ever wanted in a woman. We ought to get married someday.'"

Coretta dismissed this. "You don't even know me," she said. But Martin knew what he wanted—a wife he could talk to and who had the same sense of dedication to racial equality that he had. Coretta clearly was that kind of person.

As for Coretta, her first thought when she met Martin was how short he was. As she got to know him, though, she clearly understood that Martin was looking for a wife—an appropriate pastor's wife. Later she wrote, "I wasn't looking for a husband, but he was a wonderful human being. . . . I still resisted his overtures, but after he persisted, I had to pray about it. . . . I had a dream, and in that dream, I was made to feel that I should allow myself to be open and stop fighting the relationship."

So she did stop fighting the relationship and agreed to an engagement to be married. Little did she know that Martin had already told his mother after he first met Coretta that she was going to be his wife. And when Coretta spoke of Martin to her sister Edythe, Coretta said, "He reminds me so much of our father." That's when Edythe knew there would be a wedding.

Nevertheless, the engagement of Coretta and Martin was tough to get off the ground. Martin Sr. had his own ideas about who should marry Martin Jr., and he was not going to be impressed with just anyone, including Coretta. In truth, Martin's father, often called Daddy King, had someone else in mind for his son to marry. He knew his son was destined for greatness, and he wanted Martin Jr. to be very careful in his choice of a mate. She needed to be someone who would support him selflessly and stand by his side as a good pastor's wife.

But son Martin already was very careful in his choice of a spouse. He knew she needed to have certain qualities that would befit a pastor's wife, yes, but she also needed to be someone he fell in love with. How fortunate that it was all pulling together into one beautiful woman—the talented and gracious soprano, Coretta Scott. Martin Jr. was smitten, and he was going to marry her.

A letter sent to "Corrie" during their engagement shows much about their relationship. He starts the letter

> Darling, I miss you so much. In fact, much too much for my own good. . . . My life without you is like a year without a springtime which comes to give illumination and heat to the atmosphere saturated by the dark cold breeze of winter. . . . O excuse me, my darling. I didn't mean to go off on such a poetical and romantic flight. But how else can we express the deep emotions of life other than in poetry? Isn't love too ineffable to be grasped by the cold calculating hands of intellect?

He was in love. Then the letter goes on to discuss the latest book he read in such a way that it's clear he knew he'd found his intellectual equal in this woman. He signed his letter "Eternally Yours, Martin."

But Martin still would have to handle Daddy King. And Mother King too. She was a graduate of Spellman College, and she was going to make certain her son married an educated woman at the very least. Her son, after all, was so gifted that he had started college at age fifteen.

When finally the elder Kings met Coretta, Daddy King grilled her as to her seriousness in her relationship with Martin. He let her know that a singing career would be out of the question if she were a pastor's wife. He also let her know that Martin had plenty of marriage opportunities.

Coretta remained quiet and respectful until the elder King told her that his son had "a lot to offer."

"I have a lot to offer too," she said politely.

After seeing with their own eyes that their son was serious about Coretta, the King parents were determined to meet the Scott family. They started with Edythe. They took her to lunch to quiz her about the relationship between her sister and their son. Edythe assured them that her sister was a catch who didn't need to marry their son.

Daddy King finally came around. Maybe he was worn down. Martin assured his father that he intended to marry Coretta, and he intended to finish getting his doctorate after he and Coretta married. And finally he had his father's blessing.

Coretta and Martin were married by Daddy King on the lawn of Coretta's parents' house. The couple started their married life together in Boston, both of them completing their graduate degrees. Then they moved to Montgomery, where Martin accepted a call to be pastor of the Dexter Avenue Baptist Church. Soon after that was the Montgomery bus boycott, kicked off after Rosa Parks refused to give her seat to a white man. The local, unknown Dr. King now became well known as a leader and a voice of reason in this movement.

The next years for Coretta were full of the joys of having four children— Yolanda, Martin Luther King III, Dexter, and Bernice. But there were also the frightening events that came with having a husband who was a leader of a controversial movement. Coretta felt honored and humbled that she and Martin were part of something larger than themselves, with events that would prove to be historic. But she was also a wife and mother with the concerns any wife and mother would have.

Martin started getting harassed and arrested for no reason or with trumped-up charges—and it happened frequently. By the time of his death, he would be arrested twenty-nine times and once was pulled from prison by Attorney General Bobby Kennedy himself. Anonymous phone calls with death threats were constant. In Atlanta, while signing a book he'd written, Martin was stabbed by a woman. The King house was firebombed with Coretta, their first baby, Yolanda, and a friend inside, though miraculously they were uninjured. It was all very frightening. But it all the more strongly instilled in Coretta the belief that the movement was of utmost importance.

Martin would write about his wife, "I am convinced that if I had not had a wife with the fortitude, strength, and calmness of Corrie, I could not have

The greatness of a community
is most accurately measured by
the compassionate actions of
its members—a heart of grace
and a soul generated by love.

—*Coretta Scott King*

withstood the ordeals and tensions surrounding the movement. . . . I didn't have the problem of having a wife who was afraid and trying to run from the situation. And that was a great help."

It was after the house bombing that a friend in the movement would observe, "That night, Coretta lost her fear of dying." Maybe so. But she never really lost her fear of Martin dying.

On April 4, 1968, Coretta returned home from shopping with her oldest child and found the phone ringing. Civil rights leader Jesse Jackson was on the line to give her the awful news that Martin had been shot and killed in Memphis, Tennessee. Jackson had been with him when it happened.

Now Coretta's first consideration was her children. Telling each of them in a way he or she could understand that their father was gone was the hardest thing. Their grief would be public for quite some time, and now Coretta would need to raise her children alone.

The Civil Rights movement, like many movements at the time, consisted of male leadership. While Martin was alive, they were fine with Coretta working by his side. Now that he was gone, they seemed to expect her to drift to the sidelines. But that's not who Coretta was, as they would soon learn.

She now was often the face of the movement. She started by almost immediately founding the Martin Luther King Jr. Center for Nonviolent Social Change (called the King Center) in Atlanta, Georgia. This organization existed to advance the legacy and ideals of Martin Luther King Jr. Coretta was so devoted to the work of the King Center that her children affectionately called the organization her "fifth child." All four children would grow up to be activists like their parents.

In 1974, on a Sunday morning in Atlanta, Coretta's mother-in-law, Alberta King, started to play the organ for the morning service at Ebenezer Baptist Church. Daddy King was the pastor there. All of a sudden, a young black man jumped up from the pews and yelled that he was "taking over." He pulled out two pistols and began wildly shooting with both hands. It was ninety seconds of pandemonium before men from the choir could pull the shooter down to the floor and disarm him as he tried to reload. They held him until the police arrived.

Later they would learn that the shooter claimed he "hated Christians" and that voices in his head that he felt were divine instructions had told him to kill Daddy King. But Mrs. King was closer to him, so he shot her instead. She was killed, along with a deacon, and one more church member was badly wounded.

Coretta was horrified by this senseless shooting of her mother-in-law. It was shocking that a seventy-year-old woman would be gunned down playing the organ in church, only a hundred feet from where the woman's son was buried. And that she was Martin Jr.'s mother, in the church where Martin Sr. was the pastor. It was almost too bizarre and terrible to fathom.

The shooter was convicted of first-degree murder and received the death sentence. That was later changed to life imprisonment, in part because the

King family requested it. Even in such a personal situation, the King family was against the death penalty. Daddy King would always be known for saying, "I cannot hate any man."

Coretta Scott King continued working at causes for the rest of her life. She never picked up her singing career, though she considered recording an album of freedom songs for history's sake. But her many other responsibilities—especially at the King Center—kept her from getting to it. She authored books. She won awards. She traveled the nation and the world speaking on behalf of peace.

She worked hard to help women and children who were poor and disenfranchised, mostly by working against government budget cuts that would hurt them. She said, "I must remind you that starving a child is violence. Neglecting schoolchildren is violence. Punishing a mother and her family is violence. Discrimination against a working man is violence. Ghetto housing is violence. Ignoring medical need is violence. Contempt for poverty is violence."

She also worked for many years to have her husband's birthday made into a national holiday, and finally, in 1983, President Ronald Reagan signed a bill to do that very thing. Now, on the third Monday in January, we commemorate the birth of the great civil rights leader with a federal holiday.

Coretta Scott King suffered a stroke in August 2005, and it left her paralyzed. In January 2006, while in Mexico receiving treatment for complications from the stroke, she died in her sleep. She was seventy-eight years old.

Condolences from all over the world arrived for the family of Coretta Scott King, and ten thousand people gathered for her funeral in Atlanta. Per her wishes, she was buried next to her husband at the King Center.

The old saying goes "Behind every great man is a woman." But in this case, there was a great woman standing next to a great man, not behind him but shoulder to shoulder. And when the man left this world, the woman worked even harder than before to make the world better. That is Coretta Scott King's legacy.

◉ Think...

    1. Coretta's mother believed in education so much, she did something highly unusual for a woman at the time. What was that?

    2. How did Coretta meet her future husband, Dr. King?

    3. What did Coretta's children call her "fifth child"?

◉ Imagine...

Coretta had hard times that many of us will never have, including the murders of her husband and mother-in-law. Do you have special Bible passages that you have memorized and can hold in your heart in difficult times? If so, which? If not, find and commit to memory a special passage of Scripture.

◉ Get Creative!

Many women in this book, including Coretta, were fans of singing spirituals. Do some research on spirituals (you can hear them sung on YouTube and in recordings in your library). Pick one spiritual that truly speaks to you and write the words out. Feel free to do as the freedom workers did and change a few words to fit your own situation. Now memorize your spiritual. Can you sing it to others?

14

Wilma Rudolph

(1940–1994)

 My doctors told me I would never walk again. My mother told me I would. I believed my mother.

Wilma Rudolph

The child had worn a metal leg brace for most of her young life. In all her early memories, she watched her athletic older brothers and sisters play and run and compete in sports events at school. She watched her brothers put up a basketball hoop in the yard, and she watched her brothers and her sisters dribble the ball and shoot hoops. But she could not participate. Not only that—the doctors at the blacks-only hospital fifty miles away did not hold hope of the child ever walking.

But her mother had a great faith and believed otherwise. This baby had been born early and weighed only four and a half pounds at birth. The doctors had warned her parents then that the infant was not likely to live. But she did live. It was a miracle.

And then at age four, the child contracted polio. She survived that, too, but lost the use of one leg. It was a poor household with many children to feed, so there was no money for physical therapy. When doctors realized this family could not afford the therapy, they showed the mother how to therapeutically massage her daughter's twisted leg. She in turn taught the other children at home, and for years they all massaged their sister's leg. They did that four times a day.

And it worked. She finally could walk, with the brace. Then, one day in church, the little girl removed the brace and walked down the aisle without it. The girl truly could walk, even when the doctors had been sure she would not. Maybe not smoothly and maybe not without special orthopedic shoes, but she was definitely up and moving forward. Another miracle.

One day the mother came home from work and saw in the driveway that one of her kids was shooting hoops. It took a minute to realize that it was her girl who had just started walking. She was jumping and running. And she was barefoot.

Another miracle.

Little did Momma know that the miracles would keep on coming.

Wilma Glodean Rudolph was born in 1940 in St. Bethlehem, Tennessee, near the town of Clarksville. She was the daughter of Ed and Blanche Rudolph and the twentieth child in a lineup of twenty-two children. Of course, not all of Wilma's siblings lived in the small Rudolph house when she was growing up, but many of them were there. It was a boisterous household.

Baby Wilma was born prematurely and weighed in at only four and a half pounds. She was born into poverty, though her parents worked hard. Her father worked as a porter, and her mother worked as a maid. This was the South in the 1940s, where opportunities for African Americans were very limited. So the Rudolphs kept working and hoping, choosing to believe things would get better down the road.

At first look, some people might call their house a shack. It didn't have running water. A hand pump in the kitchen brought water into the house, and the toilet was an outhouse in the backyard. But the truth of the matter was that the Rudolph house was a home filled with positive spirit and love, anchored by a deep faith in God.

Little Wilma continued to have challenges. Around age four, she contracted scarlet fever, double pneumonia, and infantile paralysis—usually called polio—any of which could have taken the life of this frail child with little access to medical care. The polio left her bedridden until she was eight years old.

In those days there was an epidemic of polio in America. It sometimes took lives or left the person—often a child—unable to walk or move whatever area of the body the polio virus had attacked. Even the president of the United States at the time, Franklin Delano Roosevelt, had contracted polio and was never again able to walk without crutches. Fortunately today there is a vaccine for polio.

But again, this was the American South in the 1940s, and even life-or-death situations were subject to segregation. The Rudolph family could only take their child to a hospital that treated blacks, and the closest one was fifty miles away. People did not drive long distances in those days very often, even if they had a car. The Rudolfs were not so fortunate financially, so at first they used the bus. Every week, for a long time, Wilma and her mother made the fifty-mile bus trip to the hospital for medical treatment—and then took the bus fifty miles back home. They did this until they had a car to use for the trip.

Eventually doctors decided the treatments were not working, so they stopped them. They kept the brace on her leg, and they showed Wilma's mother how to therapeutically massage Wilma's twisted, weakened leg to keep it from losing more function and hopefully make it stronger. Since her mother worked six days per week to bring in money, she in turn showed her other children how to massage Wilma's leg. Four times a day, Wilma's heavy leg brace was removed so that her siblings could massage her leg for her. By the time Wilma was eight, she was able to walk with the brace on her leg.

The leg brace finally could be removed permanently when Wilma was nine. What a relief to shed that heavy thing and walk without it. She limped, of course, and she was instructed to wear her heavy orthopedic shoes. Her folks had paid a lot of money for that pair of shoes, something she did not take for granted.

But walking barefoot felt so much better. She found she was able to walk just fine without those shoes, so she could wear regular shoes to school like the other kids. Her mother had kept her home from school the years she was sickly, but now Wilma was attending school with her brothers and sisters.

When Wilma was in the eighth grade, she tried out for the track team at the all-black school the Rudolph kids attended. She didn't make the team, but her sister did. Wilma did not like the idea of once again watching her siblings do the things she wanted to do too.

Neither did Dad Rudolph. He approached the track coach to tell him that his daughters needed to be a "package deal"—that is, the coach could take both girls for the team or neither girl. The coach agreed to take both girls, having no inkling what a great decision that was going to be.

Wilma loved basketball and she excelled at it. She also participated in track events to keep her strength and running skills up between basketball seasons. Somehow she taught herself to run with a smooth, even gait, although her earlier disability should have prevented that.

Her coach nicknamed Wilma "Skeeter." Why? He said, "You're little, you're fast, and you always get in my way."

But in high school, "Skeeter" wasn't so pesky. She grew to be a good-looking, smiling young woman, lean and long-limbed, standing at five feet eleven inches. She worked hard at track, particularly in sprinting events. She kept the nickname Skeeter because she liked it.

One day, when she ran in a high school track meet held at Tuskegee Institute, Wilma lost every single race. But there was a coach there that day from Tennessee State University (TSU), a man named Ed Temple, who was scouting for talent. His female college track team was known as the Tigerbelles. And he noticed Wilma.

What did Coach Temple see in a girl who lost every race? He saw talent and heart. He recruited her to come to his summer track camp at TSU, where he could work with her raw talent.

Coach Temple ran a tight camp. If a runner was late, she ran an extra lap for every minute she was late. That happened only once to Wilma. After she ran thirty laps for being half an hour late, Wilma always showed up half an hour early. Temple noted it. He could work with someone like that.

He did indeed work with this runner with her persistent attitude and discipline, and what a good thing that turned out to be. The result was that at only age sixteen, small-town Skeeter flew to Melbourne, Australia, to participate in the Olympics—and amazingly, the girl who'd shed her leg brace only seven years before won the bronze medal in the women's 400-meter relay.

Back home, she was still just Skeeter—and still very poor. She even had to borrow a formal dress to wear to the high school prom. But she did manage to get into college at TSU and was a successful member of the track team. She was very serious about her running. This resulted in her being part of the TSU team that made it to the Olympics. Once again, small-town Skeeter was off to see the world—this time to Rome, Italy.

In September 1960, Wilma won the 100-meter race, the 200-meter race, and the 400-meter women's relay. She sprained her ankle before the relay, but she ran anyway. Pain was nothing new to this survivor of polio, and she ran through the ankle pain without anyone noticing. Wilma became the first woman in history to win three gold medals in track and field at a single Olympics.

One tense moment that truly showed the will of this runner was in the relay. Wilma was in the anchor position, which is the fourth runner of the four-person relay team and traditionally the fastest. In the handoff, unbelievably, Wilma did the worst thing—she dropped the baton. Fortunately it did not disqualify the team, but it could shave precious seconds off her time. Wilma scooped the baton up and took off after the very fast German runner ahead of her. She passed her—then she passed her teammates from TSU on other relay teams, and she finished first.

It was official. Wilma could now be called the fastest woman in the world.

The still photographs of Wilma approaching the finish line in the Olympics are so amazing that one of them was later turned into a sculpture. The images in those still photos seem to be in motion. The long, lean Wilma, leg muscles pumping, head held high, is running so beautifully that the women behind her look like they're trudging. Of course they're not trudging—but Wilma was fast. At the Olympics that year, people would say about her, "Don't blink. You'll miss her if you do."

The press loved Wilma Rudolph. The international media called her "The Black Gazelle." She was model-beautiful—tall and elegant with smooth brown skin and long legs. She smiled easily, photographed well, and was courteous and humble when the press interviewed her. "I don't know why I run so fast," she told reporters. "I just run." When asked what part of the Olympic wins she liked the best, Wilma responded that it was the relay because she was privileged to stand on the platform with her teammates.

After the Olympics, the team would go on to compete in Greece, England, Holland, and Germany. Even then, people flocked mostly to watch the graceful Wilma Rudolph. Mounted police in Germany had to maneuver their horses to hold back the fans trying to surround her. Wilma simply smiled and remained calm, waving good-naturedly.

By the time she returned home from the 1960 Olympics, Wilma had seen a lot of the world and how it operated. She had made friends with other people on the American Olympic team and with people on the international teams, and many of these new friends were white. For the first time, Wilma was dropped into a world without racial segregation, and she could see what that looked like. She could see that integration was the natural way of things, not segregation, and she would never again be tolerant of racial separation.

So when Wilma learned that her hometown of Clarksville was going to greet her with a parade in her honor and that it was to be handled by the Tennessee governor, a man who called himself an "old-fashioned segregationist," she insisted the event be integrated. If that didn't happen, she said, she would not attend.

At twenty years of age, Wilma got her way with no fuss. The parade on Wilma Rudolph Day was most likely Clarksville's first integrated event, all due to the sense of fair play and the wisdom of young Wilma.

Back home, the world of sports in the sixties was not the money-making machine it is today, and Wilma retired from sports and moved on. Later she would say, "When I was going through my transition of being famous, I tried to ask God, why was I here? What was my purpose? Surely it wasn't just to win three gold medals. There has to be more to this life than that."

There would be more for Wilma. Much more. She received her degree from TSU and then taught in her former elementary school. She married. She had four children and subsequently had grandchildren—all the true joys of her life.

She coached college track. She served as a US goodwill ambassador in French West Africa. She was graced with many honors during the 1970s, including being voted into the Black Athlete's Hall of Fame and also into the National Track and Field Hall of Fame.

Wilma wrote her life story, *Wilma Rudolph on Track*, and it was a bestseller. In 1977 NBC made a movie based on the book and called it *Wilma*. It starred the famous Cecily Tyson and a young, not-yet-famous Denzel Washington.

But one of Wilma's greatest joys was starting the Wilma Rudolph Foundation to help children blossom and strive to reach their dreams, no matter what the circumstances in that child's life. Wilma knew what hard work and discipline meant in her own life, and she wanted to share her vision with other children. She wanted to be the kind of encouragement in children's lives that would help them develop their own gifts. She would say, "Never underestimate the power of dreams and the influence of the human spirit. The potential for greatness lives within each of us." Her legacy would live on in the children it inspired.

She was also an inspiration to the next generation of African-American women runners—including Olympic stars Florence Griffith Joyner (Flo Jo) and her sister-in-law Jackie Joyner-Kersee. For Jackie Joyner-Kersee, it was more personal. She said, "[Wilma] was always in my corner. If I had a problem, I could call her at home. It was like talking to someone you knew for a lifetime."

Tragedy struck when, in 1994, Wilma learned she had brain cancer. It spread quickly, and a few months later she died in Nashville. She was only fifty-four. At her funeral, the Olympic flag was draped over her coffin.

Wilma Rudolph was once the fastest woman in the world, and with that title she inspired the world. But her magnetic personality, strong character, and hard-won wisdom did even more for those who came into her circle. "Winning is great, sure," she told the world, "but if you are really going to do something in life, the secret is learning how to lose. If you can pick up after a crushing defeat, and go on to win again, you are going to be a champion someday."

After her death, one Olympic teammate said about Wilma, "She was beautiful, she was nice, and she was the best." She was indeed all that. But she also had a strong sense of determination and persistence. She moved forward quickly and successfully, basking in the support of her loved ones and in the love of her God.

That is why Wilma Rudolph could say with conviction, "When the sun is shining I can do anything. No mountain is too high, no trouble too difficult to overcome."

We can all learn from that.

● Think…

1. What were the health issues Wilma had as a newborn and in her early childhood? Why couldn't she walk?

2. Why couldn't Wilma's parents take her to a closer hospital than the one fifty miles away?

3. What was the most unusual thing about Wilma's hometown celebration after her Olympic victory?

◆ Imagine…

Many great runners credit Wilma's victories as inspiration to their own experience. Is there anyone from our culture, history, or the Bible who especially inspires you? What would you ask that person if you could?

■ Get Creative!

Physical exercise is not only good for our bodies but it's known to stimulate our brain cells. What new body movement can you add to your day? If you're an athlete, set a new goal. If you're not an athlete, "become" one by walking, running, swimming, or biking on a regular basis, with a solid goal before you at all times. Be sure to enjoy it!

Now That You've Finished the Book . . .

Discuss these questions with others who have read the book. Or if you are reading alone, write your thoughts in your journal if you keep one or in a notebook.

Who of the fourteen women inspired you the most?

Who do you think you are most like?

Who would you want to be most like?

In your opinion, who had the most to overcome to achieve her goal? Why do you think that?

Do you think any of these women knew each other? Which ones? Where could they have met?

Would you like to inspire someone? Can you think of who that would be?

Do you wonder why you're here, or do you already know?

What do you think you can do for the world?

Which woman was the most single-minded in her goal? Which showed the most variety of goals?

Have you ever had something stand in the way of your goal?

If obstacles get in your way, is there anything you can take from this book that would help you?

If you could ask any of these women a question, what would it be? Why?

Tricia Williams Jackson is a Michigan writer and former schoolteacher who loves history and enjoys sharing its stories with readers.